DIARY OF
A WAVE OUTSIDE
THE SEA

The author at age four

DUNYA MIKHAIL

DIARY OF
A WAVE OUTSIDE
THE SEA

يوميات
موجة
خارج
البحر

translated from the Arabic by
Elizabeth Winslow and Dunya Mikhail

A New Directions Book

An excerpt of this book was first published in *Calque*.

Interior design by Eileen Baumgartner

Manufactured in the United States of America
New Directions Books are printed on acid-free paper
First published as a New Directions Paperbook (NDP1141) in 2009
Published simultaneously in Canada by Penguin Books Canada Limited

Library of Congress Cataloging-in-Publication Data

Mikha'il, Dunya, 1965–
    [Yawmiyat mawjah kharija al-bahr. English & Arabic]
    Diary of a wave outside the sea / Dunya Mikhail; translated from the
Arabic by Elizabeth Winslow and Dunya Mikhail.
        p. cm.
    ISBN 978-0-8112-1831-3 (p)
    1. Mikha'il, Dunya, 1965- 2. Women authors, Arab—Iraq—Biography. I.
Title.
    PJ7846.I392Z4613 2009
    892.7'36--dc22
    [B]
                                                2009000713

New Directions Books are published for James Laughlin
by New Directions Publishing Corporation
80 Eighth Avenue, New York, NY 10011
www.ndpublishing.com

DIARY OF
A WAVE OUTSIDE
THE SEA

. . .

"No, no, poetry was not on my mind when I wrote this book," I insisted to my New York publisher, "although there were some similar symptoms as if I was writing poetry—those same symptoms you experience when falling in love, like burning cheeks and smiling for no reason . . ." But my publisher insisted that my book was poetry. As I didn't want to make New Directions unhappy, and as I also felt elated to be reclaimed for (or by) poetry, I agreed.

My partner in translation, Elizabeth Winslow, had originally transformed the unbroken, prose-poetry lines of my Arabic into a poetic broken-lined English. The change seemed to deepen the poetical sense of the translation. And yet, however much prose might bear some poetry within its sentences, poetry can bear only poetry, no matter how the sentences are broken. So whether this is a poetical memoir or memoirish poetry, my *Diary*, in its traces of experiences, has drifted for a moment from the usual classifications.

Part One was written in Baghdad during and after the 1991 war and was published in Iraq in 1995. I left my country that same year, largely due to circumstances caused by the book's publication. The second part was written after I left my homeland. In the first part, I could not say everything I remembered. In the second part, I could not remember everything I wanted to say.

Now, at this moment, I feel terribly grateful. I really do not know how to thank all the wonderful people that are part of this book! I would like to thank my Iraqi friends for singing a song from the heart with me. I would like to thank my American friends for listening from the heart to our song. My wish is that one day I can invite my American friends to Baghdad's Abu Nuwas Street by the Tigris River for a *masqouf* fish; and one day invite my Iraqi friends to New York to ride the Hudson

River tour around the Statue of Liberty. I wish to invite them both to one table, wherever that should be, to exchange our joys, our wounds, and our songs.

My special thanks go to my publisher for extending my voice beyond the Arab world: to Barbara Epler for picking my voice out from under the ruins, to Jeffrey Yang for editing my work with such warmth and patience, to Laurie Callahan for always sending me a lot of newly published books. Thanks to Elizabeth Winslow for translating my work with such care, to Louise Hartung for editing the Cairo edition of the *Diary*, and to Eliot Weinberger, Robert Hass, Christopher Merrill, Saadi Simawe, Lori Cohen—to name a few—for encouraging me. I am always in need of encouragement.

I thank my husband for being able to live with a poet.

I thank my daughter for teaching me to behave.

I thank my parents for telling me that everyone in the world is worth knowing.

Many more people are on my list of thanks. I hope they know how grateful I feel.

—DUNYA MIKHAIL

PART ONE

1991 – 1994

In my childhood, I envied myself for being a child.
I thought everyone was created the way they were:
created as a child or an old man or a mother.

I was sad for my mother.
Because of her age, she could not play like me
in the sand
or jump on the bed or hide under it
or fling pebbles into the sea
to watch the ripples spread until they vanished.

So I prayed every day,
thanking God for creating me as a child.

When I grew up, I could not stop envying myself
for remaining stuffed with childhood.

I used to count dreams on my fingers
and cry, because my fingers were insufficient!
I also cried when I saw myself in photos
and I would shout:
"Take me out of the picture!"

Thousands of enormous photographs
with music cassettes
hurl through an endless expanse of memories,
and every picture is the frame of a fleeting moment.

And because I don't like frames, I break them apart
and release thousands of people
and things
and stars
and birds
and moments
to disperse into a broken ash-gray horizon.

. . .

In my childhood, I painted armies of dust
with a ribbon spread out behind them.
I painted innumerable mirrors
with my dreams reflected in them.

I painted the sea
and my creatures perishing in it.

I painted the moon
and my isolation curling around it.

I painted your departure
and the tears I shed for you.

I painted wings
so I could depart with you.

And so on.

. . .

In my childhood, my father bought a chessboard for me, saying,
"This is life—black and white."

When he was admitted to the hospital,
everything was white: the walls, the bedsheets,
the uniforms of the nurses,
the heart of my father,
and the icy coldness of the doctors.

And when I left the hospital, everything was black:
time, the clothes of the women,
the photographs, the night,
and the day.

When my father's absence grew long
I cried.

I didn't cry for his absence;
I cried for my presence!

. . .

My lover's absence also grew long . . .

and the sun
and the moon

One evening . . .
No . . . One morning . . .
No . . . I don't know . . . One waiting . . .
Death passed before our eyes, as it did every day.
I was not waiting by myself;
the river was there, too,
and the smoke that rose from the explosions
and from the cigarette of a lover
who contemplated his loneliness
like a pawn in the corner of a chessboard.

Aside from the din of time
pounding on my eardrums like an amateur musician
were the snorts of fear
and the wailing of the trees.

In spite of this, I slept
to see you in my dreams.

In vain I tried my best
to remain in the dream.

And when I awoke, I felt my heartbeat
to be sure of your existence!

Your love staggered along the riverbanks
like my heart

and then I knew
that only the dreams of a stone don't become cracked
and only the heart of a stone endures.

Others implore me
to sweep from a corpse
the dust of your days.

And I implore you to call me.
Not to reply or to appear
but because I like to hear from those I love.

When I said one day: "I love you,"
my dreams swelled from their tomb
and danced around the words.

And when I saw you one day
and you moved away
until you were farther from me than my soul,
I watched as my dreams
returned to their tomb.

. . .

Your shadow squats on its heels
on the hands of our clock and revolves.
Revolves . . . like my head . . .
No . . . not like my head . . .
Yes . . . like my head . . .

O . . . Where does the world live?
Certainly not in memory.

The streets crawl, intersecting in the veins of my hands.
The features of the city intermingle in my mind.
The names are confused
with the faces

with the masks
with the dates
with the seasons.

How can I arrange these things
in my memory?

Someone said,
"Why don't you greet people
when you see them in front of you?"
The next day, I waved my hand for a long time
but then didn't see anyone in front of me!

. . .

Memories swarm around me like buzzing flies.

Every sorrow and mistake adds up
to a tally of daily ruination.
And nothing is as long as memories' shadow
except the moment that transforms
wood into *rebab*.

My mistakes were drawn like butterflies.
Light was projected onto them
to make them burn.

I stepped back.
The mistakes appeared like a wavy vision
beating against the shores of the seven senses
so that the pages dispersed and gathered and burst
with intuitions and questions.

We remember some things that have been lost
not through carelessness
but from their own pitch-black light
like a flower dying from too much fragrance.

V

And the darker it becomes,
the clearer the vision grows.

Roads
trees
rivers
windows—
these things are not acquainted with me,
but I know them well.
They are like tears falling
at a sudden, false shadow.

The song goes:
If the earth were square
we could curl up and hide in its corners
but the earth is round
so we must face it.

Did you know that I was flying?
My wings have sprouted—Look!

I rose higher and saw an eraser
pass along the horizon.

And in the crucial moment when heaven and earth met,
the confused soul emerged
from the earth's decaying corpse
to float in the kingdom of nothingness.
But before arriving, it got caught in the clouds
so that space was filled
with its alienation, dreams, and memories,
pouring down, mistaken for rain.

In the moment of impact, the head disintegrated
so that a million birds were released from its cells
over a sea of brokenness.
The waves like kites released from their strings

Λ

flew over the sprawling stars.
Perhaps this explains what binds the stars to the darkness.

"I saw stars suspended
like the hanging candelabras in a mosque,
then I ascended to the heavens
in the blink of an eye.
It was a sky of smoke.
On the left I saw a magnificent tree with leaves on it,
and on each leaf
a name."

The leaf with my name on it dropped from its branch
in the shape of a bird.
Other leaves, some green and some yellow,
dropped from branches
with names you know
and names you don't know.

. . .

Which is the way back to earth?

Birds in the air peck at my memory.
This is where the punctures come from.
I want to place my feet on the ground,
and know the law of gravity.

Here . . . In the sky . . .
neither gravity nor memory support me.

It is an absence
of weight
thoughts
everything.

Do the dead have the right to commit suicide

and thus return to earth?

How can this be, when I am a mere soul
fluttering over unknown things
and nonexistent places?

How did all this absence burst inside me?

And how did my soul come to squander itself
in such extravagance?

I want a little earth under my feet.

Both of us (the earth and I)
believe that one has buried the other inside her.
I wonder who was buried first?

And who let the sun sit down
on the threshold of my heart
to keep it burning day and night?

Every day I adorn my soul—
sprinkle it with water
so that one day it might experience peace.

Sometimes I imagine the war has ended
and life creeps into the foreheads of the corpses
for an instant.
One instant is enough,
a moment
the size of a bullet.

Has the war really stopped?

O . . . Is there enough space in life for all this gasping?

Has the war stopped?

What will we do now
without enemies?

. . .

I wander among the ruins
like a word in the dictionary
roaming in search of its meanings
in a language without verbs.
I am a verb of the past,
trying vainly to change to the present tense.

They said,
"Behind every window,
no matter how small,
a horizon can be seen."

Ever since I heard that, I have been drawing windows
that open out to nothing.

I saw the sparrows writing in their diaries.
They describe how they have subsisted on my heart.
They say that one grain of love
is enough to survive on forever.

I open the window of my life.
All the sparrows fly away.
They go to the war
to nest in the helmets of the slain,
helmets full of memories
and moonlight.

In war, memories shrink back in fear.

I hold my homeland in my palm.
I spread out my hand.
There is nothing but gasping,

a bullet in the flesh of wishes,
a crushed dream.
When my time chases me,
I hide.
But whenever it runs away
I follow it
to gather from its desolation
this scattered bird
who shares my trembling.
One wish is enough
to leave the doors open to the day
and name the sun as Sun.
One wish is enough
to make the universe rise like a vapor
from the heart.
In the beginning, wishes used to carry me
and whirl me around.
Now I carry them and whirl with them.
We whirl . . . we whirl . . .
And so do the nights
and my wishes remain wishes.

. . .

One cold morning, I knew it was the day I would die.
So I prepared myself completely for death.
I finished my last poem
and arranged my coffin
and bought flowers to be thrown on my grave.

Death and I—
we both like flowers.

I said to myself,
"Have I forgotten anything before I die?"
I remembered that I had not put the chessboard away
and I was afraid this would make the king angry with me.

So I arranged each piece in its place on the board.

At dawn the next day, I saw the chessmen running for shelter
and I thought, "Why should we hide in shelters
when the sky is clear?"
We curled up and hid in a corner
without knowing if we shivered from cold
or from fear of chemical weapons.

In a white room, the snow inside us
touched the heart's darkness.
The walls rose around us bit by bit
and the ceiling lowered above our heads.
Everything merged together
and rolled into the shape of a missile
aimed at my head,
which had transformed into a wastebasket.
And before I could apologize to the missile
for the vast emptiness inside my head
my brain tissue flew out like wounded sparrows
carrying my memories.
The sparrows stood in a triangle on my head
like a tombstone.

In a narrow corner of my heart
I touched a moment
that was a whole life.

Lightning struck inside and outside; shifting sands
spread between one heartbeat and another.

—But I didn't find a trace of your footprints.
—Did you forget that I had to be carried?

. . .

When the countdown began

and the fortune teller told me it was the Day of Judgment,
I wondered, Why haven't the things
my grandmother said were foretold in books
happened yet?

Wasn't it necessary for history
to empty its gun before Judgment Day?

And why on earth didn't my grandmother tell me
our days would be pressed into tin cans
and people would be squeezed into small spaces
like sardines in a can
and the advanced technology of the Allies
would try to eat us
instead of canned food
and "zero hour" would be announced
and the "r" shivers from *bard* (cold),
the "r" that separates *hub* (love) from *harb* (war).

This occurred on 1/17/91
at dawn or during the night.
It was not a nightmare,
and the moon—by virtue of its location near the planes—
witnessed everything that fell.

Everything was falling.

And how pale the moon appeared
reflected in the Tigris that night!

The Christmas tree had not been taken down yet
even though it was two weeks into the new year—
the year already cheating us
of our 365 days.

Everything inside and outside glowed
and extinguished

like the Christmas tree.
We curled up in one corner
and the "r" trembled in our mornings
and ruins
and fires.
We were in the hands of the Allies
like a pack of cigarettes,
and the longer the minutes burned,
the more the city smoldered.
The balance between smoke and candles became a deficit.
We inhaled death,
and gazed at nothing like puppets.

I saw my neighbor the gardener
sowing gasoline in the garden.
Does fire grow?

Storage tanks were filled
with gasoline and questions
and newspapers reported
a theory of the death of the author
and the death of date palms.

Eyes were riveted to television screens
and the country was a sparrow
strangled between two fists
shaking firmly.

The announcer broadcast the news
with bubbles coming out of his mouth.
The planes pass over Echo Rock
shaking the branches.
The stars are falling . . .
The Rock repeats:
"Falling . . . Falling . . ."

The tanks were filled with gasoline,

fear, and confusion.
We went to the village of Telkaif.
The Chaldeans there were minding their sheep
even in a time of war.
In a room with no ceiling I sat watching the roosters
who fought for no apparent reason.
The Bible says: "Man is not favored over the animals . . .
both arrive at the same place . . ."

The village was smaller than a graveyard
and bigger than the planet Venus
which fell into my aunt's *tanour*
so her bread was flavored like roses.

Once again
we bow
to let war fly over us.
They sit quietly in front of their electronic screens
and press a button
to erase our torn wings
the moment before we fly over our ruins.
They press another button
and their planes scream toward us again
as if the hell their new machines have made
is not enough
to face the paradise of meeting our loved ones again.

I wonder how Santa Claus of the twentieth century felt
when he carried a sack of shells to the children of Iraq.
And how did he feel when they gave him back the sack
filled with such presents
as a mutilated finger
a red braid
a torn book
a damaged toy
a card of protest?

I wonder how the critics who linked
the theory of aesthetics with that of explosions
felt when they saw the bombs fall
over the building of the Iraqi Writers Union
and the Academy of Fine Arts;
over the Jumhuriya Bridge,
the bombs scattering the promises of students
whispered in the ears of their girlfriends
into the river;
over Al-Rasheed Street by day
and Abu Nuwas Street by night;
over the Al-Sayyab statue with his pocket already torn;
over Gilgamesh,
who was searching for immortality
among the ruins.

This evening, as the rain resembles a tear,
I think of the poets of the 1980s
who sang of their lost wings
and of my friend Huda, who said that flowers
not offered to lovers soon fade.

The hands of the clock crumbled,
leaving behind lives of darkness and ash
and broken-heartedness.
When I peeled away the brokenness
I found more brokenness inside—
the heart's beads detached
and time filled with absence.

They chant a sob . . .
I mean a song . . .

The radio says that Allied planes are dropping cluster bombs
on shelters and bridges.
I never heard of such a phrase
except as a cluster of grapes.

O life . . . a suspension bridge between two wars.

Why don't the flowers of others like to bloom,
save in the remains of our ashes?

The letters do not arrive.

The telephone does not ring.

Nothing rings but me.

What time is it now?

Is the war over?

Will they return?

Was there enough room in the sky for the birds
when the planes raided our dreams
and turned everything to flour?

It was a night of extremes.
Some of the residents could not sleep,
while others slept forever.

And when the spots of light multiplied in the darkness,
flying things lost their minds.
No one could tell if the birds had changed into planes,
or if the planes had changed into flaming birds.

Everything was shaking.
The city and the people inside the city,
the hearts inside the people,
and the people inside the hearts.
The planes circled over the capital,
pumping its residents into the villages
toward an unknown fate

and toward the questions of children
that grownups do not know the answers to.

The planes flew over Al-Tahrir Square,
filling the eyes of Jawad Salim with dismay
as his horses left the city.

The planes flew over the shelters . . .

Over the debris that collected in the shelters

Over the children who slept under the debris

Over the body parts that had been children

Over the ash the body parts became

Over the walls sprinkled with ash

Over the drops of blood on the walls . . .

In war, no one is rescued from death.
The killed die physically
and the killers die morally.

In this age of words like Missiles. Aircraft. Bombardment. Blockade.
Sanctions. Slogans.
In such an age Romeo and Juliet commit suicide
not out of love but out of anger and disapproval.

Smoke.
Smoke rises
from the burning houses
from the cigarette of an American soldier who feels guilty
from a cat's tail.

The Desert Storm drops birds of shame,

and kings smile at statues of themselves and pray:
Oil is Greatest . . .
And the rivers continue their usual flow
as if we are invisible,
always hidden under the debris.

The disaster watches over us at night
—our recurring, endless night—
like a verb with no subject or object.

And look, here we are,
trying in vain to jump over it
—over the disaster—
so that we stumble from nowhere
every time.

We become acquainted with death at the wrong time,
and no one uses their "veto."

You think, therefore you realize the disaster.

Maurice Blanchot, the French intellectual,
thought that while disaster removes the haven that is the thought of death,
and turns us from the grievous or surprising thing,
and makes us dispense with any will or movement,
it does not, however, give us an opportunity
to raise this question:
What have you done to realize the disaster?

. . .

On 1/16/93, at night, the planes returned
with their confusing air raid sirens.

In the beginning, I thought what I had heard
was the sound of memories
and the buzzing

that had been reverberating in my ears for years
had escaped into the air.

The telephone rang.
A poet's voice was on the other end:

—Hello . . . did you hear the news?
—What news?
—A plane has crashed . . .
and did you go to the printing house . . . ?
and did you . . . ?

The wailing of the planes increased
and the voice of the poet faded.

I replaced the receiver,
feeling that the sky
would inevitably crash down on our heads one day.
The planes returned to thrust their beaks into our air.
They made a hole in the walls of our heart.
Through it, you could watch the disaster.
They brought tar and cement to plug the hole,
to close it precisely.
But they could never make the desolation
that remained within it disappear.

One day, curious people will arrive
to open the hole again
and observe the remains of the collapse.

O Pilot, you have the power
to demolish a human being in the dark,
but do you have the ability to defeat the night
that descends on the heart?

Surely you can kill a man with your advanced machines,
but this does not mean you have defeated him.

Didn't Hemingway already write this?
I saw him yesterday and he said to me,
"From nature's point of view,
there is no difference between the death of a man
and the death of a leaf."

Hemingway did not believe me when I told him
about the return of the planes
to a sky still gleaming with sorrow, the planes
scattering black tears to the earth.
The earth stood frowning before the mirror.
A child pointed to its reflection and said,
"You are not the most beautiful land."

The earth had become bloated
from swallowing too many martyrs.

Abandoned by the moon,
she became despondent and began to smoke immoderately.
Human beings suffocated and kept coughing.

Smoke . . . smoke . . . smoke rises from the remains of things.

Smoke sneaks into the tombs.

When will a cemetery be invented
that is impenetrable to smoke?

The earth is suffocating
far from the smile of a child.

Neither the lightness of feathers nor that of dreams
is enough to carry it, with its glass cages.
All glass is liable to break.

The birdcage that hung from a post
in the courtyard of our house

resembled the gallows.
In the cage were sparrows that did not chirp—
I didn't know if they were mournful or mute.
One of them died after a few days,
just like that, without saying a thing.
I buried her in the garden.

And later, when I planted a red rose in the dirt as a tombstone,
I heard, to my surprise, a chirping from the flower's blossom.
What surprised me even more was how,
when I proceeded to pick a petal,
I saw a drop of blood fall onto one leaf.
I rubbed the petal to be sure of what I saw
and my hands filled with feathers.

At night, I opened the door of the birdcage—
the three sparrows were reluctant to leave their place
but I encouraged them by picking them up
and spreading out my hands
to the wide open sky above.
I brought each of them out, one after the other,
as if rescuing an entire kingdom from destruction.
I gazed at the sparrows as they flew,
and was so elated that I left the cage door open
after they had returned to rest.
The next morning, I heard my grandmother say
that the cat had eaten our meek sparrows.
She complained: "They were not even safe in a cage."

So whenever I see birds in a cage
I transform into four walls.

. . .

I remember one Easter after church,
walking out from among the crowd of worshippers
toward a candle in the open air.

I stood contemplating it
until the candle melted into the shape of a child
inverted in a lap.
A person dressed in white approached me.
He gave me a Bible, saying that he saw a strange gleam in my eyes.
I replied that perhaps the candle flame caused this effect.
He suggested that I might become a prophet one day.
I remained confused for a long time
saying and doing nothing.
Whenever I saw someone I knew, I wondered,
How would they react
if the words of the man in white came true?

Since that time I have waited in vain
for an angelic revelation
to send me a message while I sleep.

My dreams or nightmares recurred:
stars trembling in the sea; a horizon
receding like an echo.

Once I saw a gigantic stone roll down from on high
and wings were scattered like a vanquished army.

Just like sleepwalkers
we go off to war
and plunge into deep garbage.

. . .

The child clenched his fist in his dream
as he heard the repeated command:

Shoot your enemies.

Shoot your enemies.

The child rose and asked his mother:

—What are enemies, Mama?
—They are those ghosts
who stand behind the line,
pointing their guns at the moon.

—But the moon is shared between us and them,
so are they firing at the part that is ours?
—Yes . . . Sometimes they hit the target
so that half or more of the moon falls,
leaving a crescent. And sometimes the moon
disappears completely.

—This means that sometimes they also hit
the half that is theirs, Mama.
—Yes, that's true. And this is called sacrifice.
They sacrifice what they have
in order to annihilate what we have.

—And what do they gain, Mama?
—They ruin our victory.

—What is victory?
—They destine us for loss.

—What is loss?
—Losing victory or winning loss.

—When will we leave?
—Leave to go where?
—To where the moon does not fall.

. . .

Yesterday, the moon fell into the oven
and was baked with the bread.

And so I made a mistake in my prayer:
Our Father, who art in heaven,
give us this day our daily moon . . .

I wanted to correct this so I said:
Forgive me for eating the moon.
I know you are everywhere,
but I wait for your song
as I wait for the missing.

Every day we write our wishes on scraps of paper
and place them in a bag.
Is it true that the devil comes each day
to take the bag to hell?
O Father, stop him! Stop him on the road,
but don't empty our wishes over us.
They are heavy,
and even if they are not,
it's enough that they make us feel that we lied,
that we lied to ourselves.
O Father, you have commanded us not to lie.

Our soldiers have grown in the fallow soil.
A few of them flew to heaven. They struck the clouds
—thinking the clouds were enemies—
with their tapered wings,
and rain fell from the eyes of the mothers.

What did you tell them after you opened heaven?

Our country sleeps standing still;
its time passes standing still;
its heart beats standing still—
so let us stand still a minute in mourning.

O my homeland, you possess an idea like a needle
(sharp, thin, and stinging).

Through your eye
history enters
and punctured helmets pour out.

Frequent tremors occur in your land
as if invisible hands shake your trees day and night.

They blockaded you and banished the oxygen from your water,
leaving the hydrogen atoms to quarrel with one another.

Shouldn't the nations be disturbed by the face of a child
who shuts her mouth and eyes
in surrender to UN resolutions?
But they only opened their own mouth slightly,
smaller than a bud,
as if yawning or smiling.

We made room in our day for every star,
and our dead remained without graves.

We wrote the names of each flower on the walls
and we, the sheep, drew the grass
—our favorite meal—
and we stood with our arms open to the air
so we looked like trees.
All this to change the fences into gardens.
A naïve bee was tricked and smashed into a wall,
flying toward what it thought was a flower.
Shouldn't the bee be able to fly over the fence-tops?

Long lines are in front of us.
Standing, we count flasks of flour on our fingers
and divide the sun among the communicating vessels.

We sleep standing in line
and the experts think up plans for vertical tombs
because we will die standing.

We are scenery lacking everything;
existing, if not for the existence of politics.

Our flowers scale the walls in dreams.

Widows dream of storks
dropping the missing down the chimney.

And orphans enter the underground tunnels
believing they are long kisses.

Every day we praise God
and we endure the spit of the devil,
then we pray for the sake of the homeland,
our lost paradise.
Every day, they fill jars with words or wars;
every day we shatter the jars.

The war merchants sell the air
and glorify medals made of tin;
and girls comb the wheat each day
and sift the clouds into bowls
so that cotton rises over their heads
just like the revolutions that rise
in a white dress, and the girls
don't know if it is a shroud
or a wedding dress!

. . .

The martyr couldn't believe his eyes
when his tomb was bombed
as he braided a garland for his beloved—
a red garland,
yet . . . on the way to heaven . . .
it turned white.
He bent toward the water with a small rainbow clutched in his hand.

In this way he makes music.
He lifts his hands to the clouds and braids her tears into a flower.
In this way he sings.

A wave breaking outside the sea.
In this way I go on.

. . .

I dream of traveling to the faraway cities
that the geography teacher points out on the atlas.

She asks me:
—What is a bridge?
—A bridge is a mother bending over her child
who has fallen with the dead leaves.
Her tear is the trembling of drenched birds.

—What is the Shatt River?
—The Shatt is a heart not occupied by anyone
though nevertheless remains torn apart
from all those who claim sovereignty over it.

Races emerge and die out, and the Shatt plays with the pebbles,
indifferent to all the wars on its banks.
Sometimes it says to itself:
"O what fools they are, constantly positioned
on my right and on my left.
Should I cast them to the pebbles,
who were their ancestors in ancient times?
This large protruding stone was once a king.
And that smooth egg-shaped one was a princess.
So when will they realize that, in the end,
they will all come to rest at my feet?"

. . .

Slivers of glass, tales, birds, and shouts
gathered around a woman in Al-Rasheed Hotel.
She was dead.

How dreary is every rock
from which your flower doesn't emerge.
O, my homeland,
how withered you are becoming!

. . .

A father wanted to do something for his children
so he sent them to the bomb shelter
and went to sleep.
He saw his children in a dream, as transparent angels
rising from the mouth of a volcano.
The blood dried in his veins from anxiety
until he became a small stone.
A child appeared and slung the stone with a slingshot,
so that it lodged into the mouth of a well
and stretched across a bottomless chasm forever.

. . .

The neighborhood children knock on the night's door
in search of a candle.

And the pawns, shoeless and dreamless,
retreat from the chessboard.

This world believes in democracy,
therefore it grants the dead
the freedom to wander the city.

I always rise from my seat as if to open the window.
Perhaps I was born to open the window,
or to wander.

Alone, I count the wars—
the trees—
that drop their fruit
in front of the children.
The children eat them and suddenly grow old.

Bitter are your fruits.
When will you raise the children
far away from the trees?

. . .

Death always longs for us.
It comes from beyond the continents.
It crosses great distances with a basket of fire in its hands.
It gives us balls of fire to play with
until we forget the meaning of the sun!

The child kept looking for a pale moon
he had seen one day through the window.
Maybe it tumbled down in its sleep (what is sleep?)
Maybe the worms ate it (what are worms?)
Maybe it disappeared with the electricity (what is electricity?)
Maybe the storm has abated.
Maybe the storm hasn't yet begun.

They said: Fill the boxes with air
(inhale and exhale and nothing).

For what and for whom are we storing the air?
Fruit does not bear our crown
and shadows do not reflect our existence.

Noise fills the place,
as if a box was opened unexpectedly,
and piles of people,
cars, and suitcases fell out

into what, we don't know
and they don't know.

What kind of enchantment transformed the city,
shouting with life and commotion,
into a sleepy princess who waits for the prince's kiss
in order to yawn again?

What kind of hands sprinkle death over the trees
so that grains of wheat fall from shivering beaks
and the bulging eyes of birds
stiffen with broken eggs?

Since they are skyless eyes, they don't see the stars
shining over a falling bridge.

The gods have turned us into idols,
but they forgot to kill our feelings
so our sufferings continue into eternity.

We don't have remains.
We . . .
We are the remains.

Where are you rushing to with your ax?

The wars multiply
and discard us.
As for the other one,
he sets off on tiptoe over the graves,
on his way to another war.

. . .

I know your hands are empty.
I know your hands have nothing to do now.
But this does not justify training them to applaud.

. . .

You are not like the night, so why does the darkness want you?

Where were you when I established the sea
and painted the sky beside it (I don't want airplanes)?

Where were you when I established your shadow
and carved my teardrop on it
so that rivers of wax flowed in the city?
The candle's shadow is trembling!

Where were you when I established a flower
and asked you to pick it for me?

Where were you when I established the universe?

In the beginning, there was only a shapeless, single-celled amoeba.
I breathed my astonishment into it
so that mighty and conflicting things flourished.
The air circled around the cell,
pressing it into an unparalleled slightness.
I saw that this was good,
and stars sparkled with my joy.
I grasped the stars
and hung them in the empty sky.
In order to eliminate the confusion
of the single chaotic mess,
I divided it
and two radiant balls rolled out.
I named them the Sun and the Moon, and gave one to the day
and the other to the night.
When I turned in exhaustion to look at my creations,
I found only futility and grief.
I grumbled and the wind blew.
I cried and the rain poured.
I breathed my dreams into the water

and fish with multicolored scales swam,
the seas overflowed with myriad kinds of life.
I gave the birds to the air and the beasts to the land.
Then I took a handful of dust
and soaked it with my tears.
I breathed into the dust
and it became a creation in my image.
I finished my scene, and I rested on the seventh day,
which I sanctified by declaring it a holiday.
I was stricken with boredom,
so I mixed the fire and air and water and earth,
and here I am smelling the odor of the debris.
I regretted all my deeds,
so I painted the flood and waited seven days more
before I freed the dove from the ark.

The waters rose until they almost engulfed
the one ship in the painting.
I ran leaving behind me a city
with steam rising from it.
But I turned back
despite the voice saying,
"Any who turn back will become a pillar of salt."

I ran away
though my feet remained in place;
and in my mouth was a strange taste
and a mysterious feeling
of dissolving into the water.

O . . . How did it remain alone,
this city, full of oil and grief?

The city's tears flowed out, bearing an inscription that read:
"Wisdom is better than weapons of war,
but one sinner destroys much good."
I said, "Then let me cancel the race of fire

and strike the water with my stick
so the water will not change into blood."

Seven days passed after I struck the water.
The oxygen atom died,
and the hydrogen atoms erupted in loud wails.
I scattered the dust like curses over the people,
who suffered under heavy burdens.
Each one bears his sin.
And I went on bearing the people—my sin—
and the burdens expanded
until clouds enveloped the houses.

When are we leaving?
When the clouds rise from the houses.
And if they don't rise?
We are expecting them to rise.

And they blew trumpets to make the clouds rise.
And the clouds rose.
Then why do they keep blowing the trumpets?

They went out—trailing coffins—
searched for a place to rest.
They complained and cried out,
"Why did we come to this world
just to fall under the sword
and have our children become prey?"
They rose to the clouds.
They rose.

. . .

How long have I been here,
riding the time machine?
In the machine I leap into the future
and find myself transformed into a fetus

inside the belly of a whale.
I will be born soon and discover the world anew.
I hope this time I will live without words—
these creatures of destruction
do not let me do anything save retreat to the depths
with the remaining aquatic races.
And it seems I will be born
under the sign of Pisces forever;
Neptune, the god of the sea, has
written his wishes on my forehead.

I adjust the machine for the distant past
to see Utanapishtim reveal the divine secret
of secrets to Gilgamesh.
He said, "O, Gilgamesh, I shall reveal to you
the secret word.
It is a secret plant. This plant—
like the spines in the depths of the sea—
reach out your hands and take it
and you will gain eternal youth."

I saw the mistress of the water
who gave me the secret word
by placing an oyster shell to my ear
so I could hear the code of the sea.

She said, "I wanted to bring you the sea,
but it was busy with hurricanes
and embracing the drowned.
The sea was in a drunken stupor
from sipping the moon drop by drop.
I stole its sound from its hiding place
in the heartbeat of the oyster shell,
and brought it to the escaping wave."

At the surface of the water,
the whale snatched the plant of joy out of my hand,

and vanished into the sea-depths.
But the whale forgot a grain of sand on my forehead,
left behind when it kissed me
beneath the conjunction of Jupiter and the sun
as it gave me the single secret word.

The shell cast a shadow in my ear
that whispers a new secret every day.
One evening, the shadow told me that the point
is the origin of the world.
After the effects of the enchantment
that had frozen its soul wore off,
the point yawned and woke from its slumber.
It saw infinite space; it moved and left the mark
of another, contrasting point behind it.
The point turned back and an attachment—
that is, a straight line—
extended between the two points.
In the middle of the straight line sits a central power
surrounded by a halo of light
and held aloft in splendor and awe
by eight sacraments.

. . .

Some clever points discovered half of the secrets,
while the remaining secrets were left untouched.
The central point is protected by these remaining secrets;
the curtain falls at the moment of disclosure.
Revelation of the secrets
is the end of the decisive line between the light and the dark,
and the alternation between night and day.
Instead, the night will possess half the globe
(the half that has turned its face away from the sun forever)
while the day will always have the other half.
The residents of the first half will be called
the people of fire or darkness,

and those of the second half
the people of light or paradise.
As for those who stand on the line
between the dark and the light,
they are in purgatory until they are allowed
(by a simple puff)
to move slightly to one side or the other.
A magical power froze the soul of the point,
and another, opposing power breathed spirit into it,
making it yawn.
Yawning is the beginning of waking
and the beginning of life.
Movement follows and leaves a trace.
The first movement of the point leads to annihilation
because the displacement is equal in this case to zero,
therefore the moment of annihilation will be at the moment
when the point meets its opposite (or trace)
and leaves electromagnetic waves behind.
The chemist Paul Derek confirms this, saying that
the electron and its opposite are born together
at the same place and same instant,
and they die together whenever and wherever they meet.

I thought of this when the Allied forces dropped
eighty-eight thousand tons of bombs
on the land of the two rivers
and made a spectrum in the air
at the speed of light or fear
leaving an indestructible energy.

It was an idea that met its opposite
and became rays of light
that destroyed people and stones.
Yet, the destruction of matter released a greater energy
that confused their experiments
and transformed our photographs
into negatives.

It is said that the energy of the dead is zero,
because the dead cannot open their mouths
or move their lips.

We are dead but have energy.
That is the difference.

As for these holes from the bombs
in our spirits and our stones,
they are not mere empty hollows. They are exactly like
that hole which is made by the negative electron
when a positive electron appears at the same moment.
This gap made by electrons or bombs has an existence
that can't be easily abolished. When the gap clashes
with the walls of memory, a blazing spark is produced,
which flashes counterclockwise.

Straight lines intersect, causing every point to split
into many similar points. These points meet
and shake their small heads in space.
As for the central point, it enters the cloud's room,
from which the cosmic courses are drawn.
It bursts into tears from the terrible shock—
rain showers down and the drops collect, covering the world with water.
Blocks of dry land spring up here and there; rainbows appear.

The points spread (some on the water and some on the land)
and begin to act like each other
or differently, as directed by the rays of light from the cloud's room.
The points continue in their determined courses
until they bump into each other. Then they stop
so their remaining energy (their ashes) doesn't perish
but materializes instead, passing through the sieve of light
so that its new role is determined by the amount light it emits.

I toy with the machine so that pictures appear
and numbers accumulate.

The numbers are strange.
We cannot count them but can use them for counting.
What is the meaning of infinity?

The geometrical forms have definite dimensions
but they all become circular in the dream
when the soul departs its home (the body)
and wanders about in a world with no end and no dimensions.
The soul goes backward and forward
to see events before they take place
(by minutes, or days, or centuries). It glimpses the future,
unveiled by its delicate vibrations.

When I moved the time machine's lever to the year 1991,
it began to shake severely and seemed as if on fire.
My God! It is falling
down
under the debris.
It is breaking up
and taking phases
and photos
of the events
like the moon in the palm of my hand.

The moon is round (and sometimes shaped like a bow);
so are the aspirin pills
the raindrops
the wheels
the bubbles (before they burst),
but only the zero achieves infinity.

Note that if any figure (except the zero)
is divided by itself, the result equals one.

In other words, if you suppose that A is any neutral figure (except zero),
then A/A = 1.

While zero divided by zero equals infinity.

I wish I could turn the time machine's indicator to the year 0,
but the disaster has ruined everything
and the machine can no longer travel either into the past
or the future. It is broken.
It has stopped at this critical point in history
when displacement is equal to zero.

. . .

In a carriage pulled by a line of smoke, I reached
into my grandfather's beard.
He would touch it whenever he heard the whistle of a train.
"Don't wander off too far
or a strange plant will swallow you," he told me.

I left his beard for a Ferris wheel
where I learned that the world is round like my fear.
My mother heard the train's whistle and said
that her father had wandered too far away.
I jumped from her lap and went searching
for the strange plant that had swallowed my grandfather.
I met the chasm face to face.
It convinced me that I was wrong,
that I didn't understand events until they took place.

The capsized boat looked like the river's grimace.
But when I left I became one of the boat's teeth
and the river seemed to be smiling.
I saw all the countries on the map
and took them by the hand.

A bird defecated on the map
before I covered it with white ink.

How many clouds do I need

to rain my wishes over the cities?

How many emigrations do I need
to create verses?

Why am I blamed for departing from mirrors
that reflected what I didn't like to see?

I wonder what will happen if the mirrors think
to look at themselves!
Will they, for instance, jump in the river?

Thus our lives pass away
like ripples in water, the ripples
in a cardiograph. The phrase
"How are you?" appears at each curve.

I don't turn the other cheek when struck
because I am absentmindedly watching the moon
fall like a tear.
The bow is taut enough to release songs from within
and I have launched the earth far away.

Something rolls on the horizon and attracts the minerals.
An exhausting flash buries innumerable people.
Engines run faster than eggs whipped in our dreams.
Weapons with dark wings crash into the nether world.
Gas masks dangle in the isthmus.
Mouths open and close like the bolt of an old wooden door.
Beards play dominos with the seven cave-sleepers
and await a miracle.

During the journey, I spent some time reading
a stone tablet of Deuteronomy:
The Lord shall bring a nation against you from afar,
from the ends of the earth as swift as the eagle flies;
a nation whose tongue you shall not understand;

a nation of fierce countenance who shall not regard the elderly
nor show favor to the young; a nation
who shall eat the fruit of your cattle
and the fruit of your land until it destroys you
and leaves you neither corn, nor wine, nor oil,
nor the increase of your kind
nor the flocks of your sheep
until it destroys you;
and the nation shall besiege you at all your gates,
until your high and fenced walls fall.

I was rowing a boat
when the carriers of a coffin crossed the river.
And the water flowing from the heights stopped
and stood as one block.
I saw them lift a stone and say
it was a souvenir of the water
that parted before the coffin.
Once they set foot on dry land again,
the water returned to its place and resumed its usual flow.
I saw them digging near a palm tree
that was bent from disease.
They lowered the coffin into the darkness,
then covered the hole with the stone
(a souvenir of the water).
Some dates sprinkled down on the tomb
as if to sweeten the bitterness of death.

A man approached the stone
and shifted it a little.
He began talking to the dead woman
who was busy giving answers at her trial in heaven.

The earthly man said,
"You, who were born from my rib,
wouldn't it be more appropriate for you to return to my body
rather than return to dust?"

The heavenly voice said,
"Why did you kill yourself
before the appointed date?
And what will the Angel of Death do now?"

The earthly man said,
"Why did you have to do that?
If you'd had patience for a few minutes
I would have filled your hours with rainbows
and at your touch colorful streams would have bubbled up
from under the gardens."

The heavenly voice said,
"Who showed you the way
to the place where there is no disease,
old age, boredom, or destruction?
Who?"

The earthly man said,
"We had our feasts and the stars that we lit on the tree.
Why have you switched off the lights
and drawn a curtain over life?"

The heavenly voice said,
"Why have you provoked the seas into flooding,
made the sunflower turn toward the moon,
and the mountain revolt for the sake of a slow ant
who has not yet reached its peak?"

The earthly man said,
"I remember those good days I spent in paradise,
before I knew you
and was expelled because of you.
I wish I hadn't listened to your words,
for what have I gained but misery?"

The heavenly voice said,

"Why did you tempt your man
to leave his good land?
It was because of you
that fire disturbed the order of heaven."

The earthly man said,
"Am I one of Prometheus's creatures
that angered the gods,
so they gave me this 'woman'
who cast my wings against the wall
and descended (with my weight)
into the hole?"

The heavenly voice said,
"The bird was created before man,
so the latter should last longer than the former.
Why then have you violated the rules of nature
and exchanged all the gifts for wings?"

The heavenly voice carried the woman of wings
to the heights
while the earthly man entered the tree
to grow himself a new rib.

I stared at the sky.
A seagull was the constant companion of my boat.
It reminded me of Jonathan, the seagull who left the flock
to live alone on the heights overlooking the sea.
He discovered that gulls are hindered from flying
from fear and the oppression of society
limiting their lives.

Yet, the seagull Jonathan grew without aging,
and his flying ability increased wonderfully
until he reached the sky.
Thank God when he flies.
Thank God when he falls.

I felt cured of all illness
while watching the seagull spread his wings in the air,
and my burdens dropped away as I rose with the bird.
I saw kings portioning out the earth
among themselves by lots, and this reminded me
of dividing things with my younger brother
when I was ten years old.
We tossed for it, "heads or tails,"
and when the coin landed one of us would win
some worthless things.
Once I threw the coin so high that it disappeared
and didn't return to the small space
between us.
I felt a unique comfort,
the relief of getting rid of the coin's resonance.
It flew away
and I gained my freedom.

With a voice louder than the calls
of water vendors in the streets,
I spelled your letters:
F-R-E-E-D-O-M
(cold water!).
And the hills stopped blocking the telescope's view,
and the sail filled with air. Only the sail was dry—
the rest of the world was covered in dew.

I reversed the lens of the telescope
and the birds appeared to be closer.
The sky became the lens of my telescope.
(Did the angel Gabriel think
that the birds had fallen into my sky?)
The trees appeared farther away.
They became lines, then points.
The hunter's bullets were shot into the air,
but nothing interrupted them.
My telescope was the only rifle directed at the birds.

But it was a rifle that shot silent, transparent visions.

A realist painter in the background shook his head,
puzzled as he replicated nature.
On the canvas, there was a huge bird
and an extremely tiny tree.
He began to think of an innovative painter
who said that nature imitates art.
I felt pity for the realist, who was going insane
staring at the new dimensions, so I reversed the lens
and made the trees look nearer
until they appeared their natural size
and were threatened once again by the chattering of birds.
The birds were threatened again by the rifles of hunters.

Before the interference of reality,
the trees lived exciting lives
and escaped the silence of generations.
When they turned into points, for instance,
they entered the Book of Judges
and ruled over the letters as if on sublime green thrones.
They said to the olive tree, "Reign over us."
But the olive tree replied, "Shall I leave my oil
for which I am honored by God and man,
just to be promoted over the trees?"
And they said to the fig tree, "Come and reign over us."
But the fig tree replied, "Shall I forsake my sweetness and my good fruit,
just to be promoted over the trees?"

Then they said to the vine, "Come and reign over us."
But the vine replied, "Shall I leave my cheering wine,
just to be promoted over the trees?"

I emerged from the Book of Judges thinking,
"Shall I leave my freedom,
just to be promoted over human beings?"

. . .

The boat rocked and almost capsized
because Zeus let a strong storm escape his magic box.
He rounded up his followers to discuss with them
the means of exterminating the human race.
He rejoiced at their suggestions, which included
floods
lightning
thunder
wars.
He pointed to the decree of war
and ordered them to implement it.

The creatures gathered in one spot, trembling.
To Zeus, looking down from his great height,
they looked like black dots.
His followers typed at the speed of the airplanes
attacking the earth.
The ground staggered under the explosions like drunkards.
In the morning, to celebrate his victory,
Zeus drank the sea and ate the nymphs.
In the evening, he excreted a great garbage of resolutions
that attracted a swarm of flies.
He had beaten the pelicans with his stick,
turning them into wild bats, foretelling who was to come.
The bats released fearful shrieks
whenever anyone tried to leave their place.
Thousands of people were killed daily
by thousands of shrieks.

Someone heard rattling underground,
and as he put his ear to the earth, he realized
it was only a shell.

In one of the compartments was a huge spiderweb
with human bodies and intestines stuck to it.

Zeus came and put a frame around the web for inspection.

In another compartment was a huge fishbowl.
The fish were hung by their fins along lines fixed to the ceiling
because Zeus did not like it when they swam free in the water.

In his spare time Zeus kept himself busy
cutting the stars from the sky
and sticking them onto chests and shoulders.
He busied himself with this hobby so much
that eventually the sky lost all of its stars.

His tigers paced in their cages.
They purred in the night as they devoured the spoils,
and in the morning when Zeus passed, they mewed.
These tigers gave lessons on the art of domestication
before a portrait of Zeus holding a whip in one hand
and gold in the other.

The snake laid many laws on his black obelisk,
for each word Zeus uttered was but a snake's egg.

He had a magic mirror. Whenever he looked at it,
his image was reflected in every direction.
Thus he was seen everywhere at the same time.
He heard everything at every moment,
and if he muttered a roaring curse a catastrophe occurred.
And if he pointed to the light and said it was darkness,
the light disappeared from light.

He clothed some of the golden remains of his creatures
and made them scarecrows on a farm.
How lonely these scarecrows felt,
for nobody approached them!

Whenever he sent one of his thunderbolts,
the congregation made their offerings:

gold
silver
sons.
They commemorated the anniversary of the thunderbolt
by holding annual public celebrations.

Some human skeletons stumbled on the way to him
and he used them to play music,
squeezing songs out of their hollow figures.

Before doomsday, Zeus sent one of his relatives (Prometheus)
to steal fire from hell. Prometheus returned with the fire, trembling.
Zeus condemned the thief of fire to be burned to death.
Then, he gave the people volcanic cinders, blazing here and there, as a gift.

The masses emerged with fire still on their clothes,
hailing the fires and those who had built them.
As Zeus toured the heavens, the gods bowed
and climbed on one another's shoulders
to help him finally reach the devil.

Once he put hell in his pocket
and descended to cast the sparks of hell over his people.
He extended his hand in greeting
and rain fell on it. A madman shouted
that a cloud was urinating on his hand.
Zeus ordered that the cloud be burned in front of the people
and scattered over the sea.
And when the waves churned with sorrow
he surrounded them with barbed wire.

. . .

On the seashore was an enormous shell
that contained the protoplasm of poetry.
Someone brought it to me
and linked the essence of my life

with its invisible thread.
I felt like a kite, looking at the world from above.
Like any child, little things make me rise or fall.

That shell of poetry drew me from or into everything
and let me do nothing but play with it and glorify it.

I have tried many times to rid myself of its magnetic power
and its deadly effect on me:

First, I tried yoga
to empty my mind,
but the shell exploited even this void,
turning the nothingness into something related to itself.

Second, I sat with a group of women
and let their voices intermingle with the chattering water
that hums in my ears continuously,
but I heard nothing of their talk
because my mind was a runaway gazelle.

Third, I announced my repentance
and confessed to the priest who said, "Confess more."
I confessed, "I have been led into temptation."
He made a special sign over my head
and asked me to pray the Act of Contrition.
He did not know that the prayer with its isolationist rite
does not differ from the act of the shell
for which I was contrite.

Fourth, I tried to roll the shell on the sand,
but its heavy core and my repetitive action
made me feel like I was moving the rock of Sisyphus.

Fifth, I resorted to a fortune-teller,
hoping that he would tell me
when the thread would be cut.

He murmured some ambiguous words
and looked at my palm, saying
that one deep line was surrounded
by some scribbles of feeble lines.

Sixth, I picked up the shell
to throw it back into the sea,
but I was awed by its overwhelming magic and beauty,
seized by its splendor as if seeing it for the first time.

Seventh, I entered the Bermuda Triangle,
thinking the shell might disappear in the Triangle's vibrations,
but then the Triangle became an enormous shell too
and trapped me inside.

When my attempts failed, the unknown came
and locked the door to imprison us, the shell and me,
and the sound of the key revealed
that escape was only an illusion.

Yet the shell, like a spaceship, carried me
to a planet full of pearls and sea herbs—
a watery planet with amoebic cells
of various shapes and sizes.

Can you paint rains that don't fall
and winds that don't move?
That is what I saw there.

I saw precious stones of unique brilliance
and paper suns overhead.
There were rivers everywhere
that didn't need bridges or anything else
to be crossed.

As for the people of the planet,
they carried perforated pitchers filled with water from the rivers.

Though they knew it was futile, they had to continue
carrying their pitchers from the rivers each day.

I laid down on the water for a short nap.
I dreamed of wandering around the earth
and talking to people about other planets.
I told people I was dreaming
and could see them only through this dream.
I told one that I lived in a big shell
and entered that place whenever I fell asleep.
He said that I had already woken.
Yet I went on and told him about my life over there
and that I am now here only as long as the dream persists.
He injected me with a syringe.
I didn't object for the pain of dreams is not real
and would end when I woke.

There, on the other side, volcanoes of water burst from the shell
exposing depths of light and dark.
Then they subsided
and flowed down to one of the streams.
Between each step are springs,
and when you walk the entire place becomes a fountain.

The layers of air in the shell
exist especially for children—
those who grow up cannot live inside it.
Children who don't understand laws
and cannot do anything well
except play
and release balloons and questions.
They go on and on and never wait for answers.
They roll the mercurial songs forward
then get bored and leave them in
neglected communicating vessels that lose
their character because they contain unstable songs.
They shoot at the rainbow with their arrows,

and vivid music with the value and splendor of silence
begins to play. They have strange eyes
that can see the smallest things,
even atoms, without effort or a microscope.
With a look, stones roll down
and everything they touch turns into flowers.
A flood of flowers has been carried
from the shell to paradise.
They descend to the river to renew their leaves,
which reflect on the water and fly off their hands to the horizon.
They wave their transparent handkerchiefs
and ultraviolet words emerge.
Their hands rise from the water as if they are about to drown,
though as soon as a rescuer reaches them he realizes
that their hands never know how to cling
even to a straw.
Their hands are always just like this,
raised as if to greet eternity.
They walk absentmindedly on the water
and return empty-handed.
Children discover the world as if they have just arrived,
and the next day they discover it again.
They have a stick of myrtle but they don't point it at anything,
because they either can't see borders
or there is nothing constant at which to point.

Shadows of ancient times are drawn on the walls.
I passed in front of the shadows
and they rose from their long sleep
to greet me with kind nods.
I smiled at them and said
that I would inscribe my own drawings on the water
to guarantee an eternal frequency.

There are no definite phrases
in the water-world of the shell.
You can say, for instance, that the clocks are broken,

when you feel the darkness will come without stars tonight.
You can say that the fences are unjustified
when you want to flirt.
You can say that this place is filled with clouds
to show you have forgotten.

Forgetfulness is my career there—
one of the difficulties I face
is that whenever I sleep
I descend in my dream to earth,
where people ask me for details
without knowing that before I met them
I did nothing but forget.
Therefore I always say to them that my dreams
are filled with clouds.

When language dies,
the people of earth bury it in dictionaries.
But language has no tomb
in the world of the shell.

One of those who crept from the water-world to land
(due to mere environmental factors)
read in the dictionary that "poetry" is metrical writing
with rhyme and rhythm. Poetry had no definition
during her previous water life.
In the shell, the goddess of poetry
used to hide poetic charges in invisible wires,
and once you found them you would be enveloped in light
and you would die.
So the amphibian realized that poetry has,
in the hands of the dictionary-makers,
shifted from gaseous matter
to liquid then to solid,
while sublimation is shifting from solid to gaseous matter
without even passing through the liquid state.

I threw the dictionary into the sea
and contemplated the words
as they grew in salty ripples.
The letters were changing places
so that *milh* (salt)
became *hilm* (dream).

The letters clung to one another
and danced in endless circles
as words appeared on a technological screen
without the interference of fingers.

As for me, I did nothing.

One day in my childhood, as I was throwing a stone into the sea,
the letters and the ripples became confused
and slipped out of one another's hands.
The letters of *bahr* (sea)
spread in complete confusion
and gathered in front of my eyes to form *harb* (war).
A great power pushed me from or into the whale—
hell was never to wake from the dream.

Many pictures pass in front of me.
They are incomprehensible, as if cut from millions of films.
Shots of people smiling at me, others looking suspiciously at me.

Someone takes my hand and pulls me along behind him joyfully;
another raises his hand and strikes my face with noise and pain.

Hands wave
or threaten
or measure a fever.

Women pass, striking their faces with their hands
while dancing around a wooden box.

Someone puts me in a glass box
from which I see a series of geometrical shapes
with black signs and dazzling lights.
Some are neutral lights but others are biased,
telling me to move or stop.
The red light doesn't change, and as I try to pass it
I am chased by whistles and strict frowns.

Many pictures pass before my eyes.

A snapshot of a pawn
waiting, one square away,
for the move that will promote him
to something else.

A shot of a snowman with a helmet on
jumping over a fire.

A shot of a branch
trembling in the eyes of a bird.

A shot from an aircraft as it swallows bombs
and expels them to earth.

A shot of the moon, exploding.

I have spent a long time here,
holding a candle that never goes out, never
melts.

This proves that I am still in the dream.

Like a haiku poem
my suitcase reduced the world into
pictures
and letters
a notebook
a pencil.
The table stayed as it was
covered with paper notes and
telephone numbers, layers
of magazines and newspapers,
and the letter opener I never had the patience to use—
my letters I would rip open as fast as I could.

I left Kasparov on the wall playing chess.
He didn't know he was the knight of my dreams
when I was a teenager. I left
all my books except *The Little Prince*,
and packed my letters and pictures
though they filled up most of the space in my suitcase.

Thirty years of my life.
I could lift it and cross the threshold with it
as I had innumerable times
coming in or going out
to school or work or the *souq*
to the Writers' Union or the Summerland Restaurant
to the cinema club or the neighbors.

As I left I knew I was forgetting something:
it bothered me to leave it behind
but I was determined not to look back,
like Orpheus leaving the underworld.
I would not look back at such a city:
beautiful and ugly
lovely and hateful
strong and fragile
hot and cold, cruel and tender,

intimate and indifferent.
I left with that one condition: to not look back.

Though I was fleeing I had to depart legally.
I needed a *mahram*, a male relative to chaperone me,
and a leave of absence from my job, at the *Baghdad Observer*.
I showed my invitation to the Jerash Festival of Culture and Arts in Jordan
to get around the *mahram* law, and Khalid M.
used his influence at the passport office.
They changed my profession from "journalist" to "poet."
A poet does not need a leave of absence from anything.

The way I fled the country was like everything in Iraq:
too hard, too easy, and exactly as they liked.

Oral laws meant more than written laws between
the two rivers—the written was not for everyone.
I wanted to move from the law of state to a state of laws;
I wanted to carry Baghdad (my Baghdad) to America,
and mix East and West together like play-doh
to make Baghdadica: freedom, abundance,
insanity, perhaps. Baghdadica
of Ishtar carrying a book with one hand
and a torch with the other.

A voice in the dust warned me not to get lost in a new land
for the sake of a dream,
lost nowhere, with no one, unknown.
Some arrive at the new land full of dreams,
but they grow tired and sleepy
and then wake without dreams.

My dreams were like the yolk of a boiled egg.
I was afraid the war would eat up the yellow
with its never-ending hunger. Life might be
somewhere else, in another place, some other place,
and I could be like memories, which do not care where they reside

or how or when or why. I could fall in a well and be forgotten.
I could close my eyes and see my own little dreams hidden there,
away from the glittering dreams of the public.
The sun could rise and set indifferently over me every day—
that is her job.

. . .

"What are all these papers?" the policeman at the Trebil checkpoint asked.
I was nervous and afraid that he might take even a scrap
from the suitcase. I told him
I was attending a poetry conference.
You know how poets talk so much at conferences
and need so much paper. He let me go free,
there, between Baghdad and Amman.
It was always a relief to be set free by an Iraqi policeman.

Hashimiya Square, in the center of Amman,
was full of suitcases and pillows.
Iraqis had set down their baggage
without knowing if this was the first stop
or the last.
The Iraqi dialect
was more common than the Jordanian
in the streets and cafés of the city.
One Iraqi joked: "What is this Jordanian doing here?!"

Without a work permit, I wrote a weekly column called "Scribbles"
for the independent newspaper *Al-Mashriq*.
The editor-in-chief M. Masharqa used to smile at me
when I turned in my sardonic columns.
He had this dream: to fall asleep for one hundred years,
then wake to see democracy in an Arab nation.
In the archive room, the staff prepared photographs
to run with the articles:

A meeting of reasonable men making plans

Leaders delivering speeches about progress and prosperity
The 50th anniversary of the United Nations
The gift of milk to a Hindu god
A new medicine for headaches
A new album by Kadhim Al-Sahir
An exhibition of African paintings and sculpture
Dinosaur fossils
Refugees fleeing their country
A frog migrating to another swamp
A cold war ending and a hot war starting
A doll buried in rubble
A crumpled map
Men shaking hands

After work I would go to Al-Feniq Club
with all the other Iraqi writers and artists.
Al-Bayatti would always be there, surrounded by young poets.
No one planned to return to Iraq.
"At least nobody here asks me for my identity card
every time I walk in the street," M. Al-Nassar once said.

One day W. Hashim took me aside:
"I am glad you are here. I want to tell you a secret."
Hashim told me that in my security folder in Iraq,
there was a question mark beside my name—for disloyalty.
"But you see," he said, "I have escaped, too."
He was loyal to them, but not loyal enough.
His poems were modern and did not glorify the war
or the government.

I drank my Turkish coffee,
and turned the cup upside down
for the woman who reads fortunes.
I wanted her to say I would meet someone
who would help me—someone, anyone.

A week later M. Masharqa said that we were invited

to a Christmas dinner at the American Embassy.
He asked me why I hadn't yet applied for a visa.
I told him that I'd heard there were too many Iraqis already waiting
who were not getting visas for any country.
The embassy dinner was my chance, he said;
he would introduce me to someone who would help me.
I told him this was an enormous favor.
"You deserve the best," he replied.

M. Masharqa introduced me to Mr. Van,
an American with Indian origins.
"Your name means 'the world' in Hindi," he told me.
"That's what it means in Arabic, too," I replied.
"You know how hard it is for Iraqis these days," he said.
He could not make any promises but he told me to bring him my passport.
Mr. Van looked like the hero in the Bollywood films
I watched at the cinema with my father as a child.
I would always embarrass my father by asking a lot of questions,
impatient to know what would happen next.
And in the end, the hero would return, and my child-
self would be relieved that he was not dead as I'd thought.

. . .

One morning I woke early to the cries of birds.
They knocked their beaks against my windows
as if they had news to convey:
My visa was ready!
I didn't know how to change my clothes that morning.
I had been sleeping in many layers of clothing
because the heater was broken. My room
was built on the roof of a building,
and the heater leaked gas that made me cough.
There was only the sun to warm me.
Mr. Van had gotten me my stamp
and I couldn't even thank him.
He wasn't there.

The flower-petal game had come true.
Pluck one for yes and one for no,
and so on. Your wish comes true
when the last petal is yes. I learned
this game from my neighbor when I was in high school.
She would pluck rose petals saying,
"He loves me, he loves me not . . ."
She was in love with a boy from the neighborhood,
but her parents would not allow her to marry him
since he was a Muslim and she a Christian.

A registered letter had been waiting for me at the post office
for more than a month. They insisted that I show my passport
in order to receive the letter.
I directed my anger at the post office
for refusing to tell me the name of the sender,
and at the American Embassy for keeping my passport indefinitely.
But with my visa and passport in hand, I received my letter
and felt only gratitude.

The letter was from my friend Lutfiya Al-Dulaimi in Baghdad,
and read: "The flowers are withering."
This was the code we had agreed upon
to get around the censors.
She was telling me not to return to Iraq.

I received another letter from Eva D., a Swedish friend.
She had interviewed me in Baghdad, and I had given her
terse, nervous answers because an employee
from the Ministry of Information and Culture was sitting with us,
listening to our conversation.
He accompanied her everywhere to "facilitate" her work.
She asked me to meet her the next day at the Babylon ruins.
There, she picked up a small stone to keep as a souvenir.
The chaperone said that the stone had no value.
Eva smiled, saying, "I can't believe that I'm walking in the same
mythological Babylon that I read about in books."

We were walking between the statues of lions and winged bulls
when she pointed to one of Saddam's statues and said,
"I wonder if people in the future will destroy his statues
like they did with Stalin?"
Thank God the chaperone did not hear her.
I whispered to her that she should not ask those kinds of questions in Iraq.

Our lunch at the Rasheed Hotel cost thousands of Iraqi dinars:
hardly the value of toilet paper.
After the economic sanctions, they started printing those bills
on the same cheap paper as local magazines.

I took Eva home and my mother cooked delicious meals for her
with the spices she had purchased from the Shorja market.
Eva dropped a valuable vase and cried.
My mother did not know how to comfort her in English.
So she gave Eva a matching vase.

We visited the newly opened International Saddam Tower
and looked through the revolving windows at a round city.
From above, Baghdad looked beautiful—green and peaceful.
The waiter brought each of us a free glass of orange juice
when he heard that Eva was visiting from Sweden.

. . .

All of my letters I kept in a paper bag.
Some I received by hand and some by mail.

Merry Christmas!
Did you receive my kisses?
I am sorry to inform you that we have stopped publishing poetry.
When I write to you, I give something away, and now not much is left.
I am sorry I could not love you the way you deserve.
Do you still keep the old Iranian coin?
I still keep the newspaper.
Your book is the first book I've ever read, apart from textbooks.

Let snow fall on your head if you do not return to Amman again.
When you hear the church bells on Good Friday, remember me.
I will love you even after death.
I wish I had a telephone to call you.
No one should know about this letter except you and God.
Soon, we will become like ghosts.
Great friends, like homelands, are never compensated.
Your poetry lacks rhythm and rhyme but contains some music.
You are sacred and unlike any other grain of sand.
All the rain in the world cannot wash out your terrible words.
We have said the rituals of the absent for you.
They are late, but we are waiting.

My photos I kept in a plastic bag
that grew fatter in Amman. I put M. Masharqa inside, too.
At the farewell party he threw for me,
he said my departure was not good for the newspaper
but was good for America.

To this bag I also added a friend
who gave me a copy of his magazine *Amman*
saying that I would get lost in America.

. . .

We crossed the sand to Petra on foot
while others rode donkeys and camels.
The dust rose and fell like our breathing,
which nearly stopped from exhaustion.
A pink fist of dust tried to strangle me,
so I frowned at it. Footprints appeared
and immediately disappeared. Faces
in the rock glared at me with frightening
and eternal stillness. I paused
by two rocks caught in a strange calcified embrace.
The rocks had human faces, and the wind
had joined their hands forever.

There were other rocks, but incomplete
with a secret beauty that did not reveal itself
to the casual traveler. Some carvings were skulls
with open eyes and toothless mouths.
These rocky bodies had their past
of dancing, wine, smiling, tears,
mistakes, complaints, ridiculous chatter.
Perhaps they still have all these things
somewhere beyond our sight.
We touched the engravings on the rocks
and entered the giant crack called *al-siiq*
emerging again like newborns, uncertain and confused.

We walked down the street to the Treasury, *Al Khazneh.*
They say that the urn will open for those who guess its secret,
making their wishes come true.
I remembered when I was a child spending all of my money
to draw a piece of paper from a bag. The bag
was in a store owned by a man we called Ammo (uncle).
I gave him five *fils*, my full childhood fortune at that time.
Ammo claimed I could win a stuffed animal
but my paper always said *boosh*,
"nothing" in the Iraqi dialect.
After long months of repeatedly losing my fortune this way,
I decided to trick Ammo. I went to him with a small
piece of paper hidden in my hand. I slipped my hand
into the bag and brought forth the little paper
to show him "bunny" instead of *boosh*!
Puzzled, he examined the paper, and said,
"But I don't have any bunnies in the store!"

. . .

In my childhood pictures, everything is black-and-white.
In a ship on a river, I wrote my first poem
about how waves are like our lives:
as one reaches its end another starts off for shore.

My cousin made a paper boat from this poem
and threw it into the river—we watched it drift away.

There is a picture of me reading the first book I loved
about an elephant who sets off for the elephant graveyard
when he knows he is going to die.

My mother in her wedding dress
looks much younger than my father.
"I didn't see him until the wedding," she told me.
"In those days husbands were like fish in the river—
you couldn't know if they were good or bad.
But, thank God, your father was the best person in the world."
Sometimes my mother wears kimonos or short skirts in the pictures.
"Those were the good old days," she says.

Once I stayed awake all night waiting for Santa Claus.
I wanted to meet him in person and not just receive his gifts.
In the morning my parents found me awake
and had to tell me there was no Santa Claus.
That Christmas I lost both Santa Claus and his gifts.

A neighborhood boy is with me in one picture
where my hair is in a braid. Once,
he handed me a letter, which read,
"You don't understand love, baby."

Here I am crying and hiding under the bed
after they cut off my braid. Somebody
kissed me on the mouth and I thought
that was enough to get me pregnant.
I even felt my belly to make sure.

Here I am with my grandmother eating wide beans
and thinking that I would definitely go to heaven
because she said there was a special place in heaven
for people who ate wide beans.

My first confession was to a priest.
I made up sins I hadn't commited
so I could have something to say.
We recited hymns in ancient Aramaic that I didn't understand.
My parents always spoke to me in the modern dialect.

In the monastery, I though about becoming a nun
just to have a place of my own, away from public responsibilities.
But I changed my mind when I found out I had to wear a uniform
and follow strict rules.

I played chess to make the pieces match my ideas and plans.
The pieces were symbols that formed possibilities with their movements,
like words in poetry. I was a chess champion for Iraq
and the hours slipped away between the black-and-white squares.
When the wars came I quit chess:
It was pointless to sacrifice all those pawns
only to protect one king.

I got lost one day on the way home from elementary school
so I went to the store where my grandfather bought me gum.
The owner asked if I was Muslim or Christian.
I didn't know.
He said he wanted to take me to a mosque or church
but I wanted to be taken to my grandfather.
My grandfather found me at the store
and bought me gum as usual.

In the square of the school, with the other girls,
I would recite the national anthem in front of the flag:
"A homeland that spreads its wings to the horizon
and wears the glory of civilization as a scarf."
My teacher blamed everything on the colonizer.
When I asked who that was, she said, "Obviously, Britain."
In biology class, my teacher taught us about amoebas.
"An amoeba has an eye and a foot," she said,
"but it doesn't have a real form.

You can draw it any way you like."
So I discovered poetry is an amoeba:
It has an eye for witnessing, a foot
for leaving traces, and a flexible form.
But doing my homework in my room
I wrote only meaningless sentences.

Some pictures I remember
were never captured by a camera:

My heart beating wildly at partings
Bombs exploding into endless vibrations
A boat swaying as the passengers disembark
A branch trembling in the eyes of a bird
Hell spilling out from a word
Air escaping the place where it had lived
Balls bouncing violently off the walls like moments of anger
A crazy woman wandering with a dead dog
An agitated monkey in a lab
Broken glass everywhere

. . .

Of all my letters, there was one that I read again and again.
It was a love letter. Of all my pictures,
there was one that I stared at for long stretches:
Mazin and I at college, with two of our friends.
Arwa and Hassan introduced me to Mazin
when he was visiting from the battlefield in Al-Faw.
He had clipped some of my poems from newspapers
and saved them.
Mazin gave me the letter when we were walking in the rain
from the College of Liberal Arts to Baghdad's Central Library.
While we walked he repeated the first line of Al-Sayyab's poem
"The Song of the Rain": *Your eyes are two palm-tree forests in early light.*

When I left Iraq, I didn't know if Mazin was alive or dead.

His picture was pale like an old moon.
He had to join the army when he graduated, like all Iraqi men.
He would come back on leave and I would skip class to meet him,
especially the boring class on national culture
that enforced the ideology of the Baath party.

I always gave him books to bring back to the front lines
where the army was fighting the Iranians.
Once I bought them at the Baghdad International Book Fair.
The day of the fair, people were so eager to get in
that they pushed down the door. Journalists complained
that they, and other writers, "needed books more than everyone else"
but could not reach any because of the endless lines.
So the government dedicated one day of the fair
for anyone with a membership card in a writers' or journalists' union.
I had the luxury of filling my cart with any book I wanted.
There were many signs with propaganda and one without:
"Egypt writes, Lebanon publishes, and Iraq reads."
"Reading is the most luxurious activity at the front," Mazin told me.

Both of Iraq's tv channels showed the exact same programs every day.
Nobody knew why there were two.
One daily program was called *Scenes from the Battle*
and showed images of dead soldiers covered with dust and flies,
scattered helmets, and body parts. You couldn't tell
which corpses were Iraqis and which Iranians.
They were mixed together, in the zone between countries,
covered with blood that was all the same color.
The next program showed images of prisoners of war.
They were lucky, though tired and dirty.
After that was a cartoon: *Tom and Jerry*.

Mazin told me stories of the soldiers.
One of them who discovered he had lost
both of his legs, turned to the nurse, and asked
if his penis was still okay.
His friend Hassan would ask questions like:

"How can we not sense the movement of the earth?"
"What was God doing before he created us?"
"What is more important, your homeland or your freedom?"
"Are stupid people happier?"
"Are the tears from onions the same as the tears from pain?"
"What is the meaning of *yas-yam* (left-right)?"
Hassan did not want to be part of a chorus, part of the herd
or even part of the march.
He said the sounds of music were like the sound of explosions
both making the same tense shape. He said
that sleep was best because it was horizontal.
It was the vertical position that caused problems.
Even being in the street required a vertical position
and that caused annoyance if not a dilemma or even a tragedy.
"Perhaps God loved birds best," Hassan said,
"because he always let them move above everything
in a horizontal way."

One day, as Hassan was walking along
in the problematic vertical form
a man in uniform stopped him and took him away.
After a long investigation they sent him to hell,
and he went. In that place, bones
are planted in the earth, skulls are
raised from the bones, and always
there is a ticking bomb
that could explode at any time.
Luckily the dove that landed on the bomb
flew away at the right moment.
Arwa could not calm Hassan
or get him to stop covering his ears
for fear of the explosion.
She yearned for the time before all this,
when there was college and no front.

Once, at college, the four of us went to an art exhibition
at the Saddam Arts Center.

Wings without birds reflected on a river;
a lonely gaze from behind a window;
a collage of a clock divided into halves
on a wall full of advertisements from another time.
In another hall there were folklore paintings
of horses, marsh reeds, and palm leaves,
of men in *kufiyas* and women in *abayas*
sitting around a big coffee pot in a black tent made of goat hair.
A special hall was dedicated to portraits of Saddam
wearing various costumes and hats:
military, civilian, Arab, Kurdish, Gulf,
a helmet, a cowboy hat.
The war was touched by the brushes of the artists
directly and indirectly
through surrealism, cubism, realism, expressionism, and abstraction.

In Al-Khadra's café, we talked about how computers were
changing the whole world except Iraq.
Personal computers were not yet allowed.
Hassan was the most excited about this technology
and told Arwa that he wished the smart computer
would replace the stupid human who resorts to weapons
and orders you to get in line
and yells for no reason
and urges you to kill people you don't even know.
Arwa asked, "What about joy and sadness and human emotions?"
Hassan answered, "Machines would gradually learn
to feel just like a human
but without his selfishness, meanness, and weakness.
Machines will be the pure innocence of human beings
without wars and ideologies and speeches and disputes."
Arwa asked, "But don't you think humans are more advanced?
At least humans have imagination. Computers
can never experience a coincidence, cannot explore
the unknown or achieve great discoveries.
A computer would never discover gravity
by having an apple fall on its head. And what about our

dreams that distinguish us as humans?"
Hassan answered, "There will be no need to dream.
We will be in the dream, in the beyond-human dream
without birth or death."
Arwa asked, "How, then, will there be life?"
Hassan answered, "There will be a new life,
to be lived by this advanced being
that does not have certainty
and is not linked to any fate
or any one idea."
Arwa asked, "What about the sensual human pleasures?"
Hassan answered, "The electronic advancement will evolve
untraditional pleasures beyond these exhausted ones.
Every pleasure will be experienced only once and never repeated,
never interrupted by outside influences.
It will be a life completely pure, without governments, enemies,
hatred, hurts, disappointments, pain,
without religion, victory, or loss."
Arwa said, "Then this is a world without art
for there can be no art in such nothingness."
Hassan said, "It's in this very nothingness that art can be created
free and transparent. We would leave this place, to go Elsewhere
to the borderless point where we emerge
like the sun and the moon. We would
ride the clouds to an uncertain place
and exchange the stars like words.
From afar we would rain down on those
who cannot see beyond their own nose.
We would look at the earth through the eyes of birds."

Mazin had tears in his eyes when he talked about the death of Hassan.
"He was scattered in the air right in front of me.
They rolled his corpse in an Iraqi flag
and took it to his parents in Zakho."
"Does Arwa know?" I asked.
"I don't know," he said.
"The last time he returned on leave,

her parents refused him when he asked for her hand.
His father said he would not give his daughter to a Kurd.
I am going to escape this war, through the north,
to Turkey first and from there to wherever I can reach."
"What if you get caught?" I asked.
"I don't care," he said. "Every day
I see death, injuries, and disappearances.
If we get married soon,
maybe someone can smuggle us outside the country."
But I refused.

After a few weeks, I realized I had made a mistake.
His absence preyed on my mind, and the Wednesday
meeting of the Writers' Union seemed bleak.
Mazin was not there. The phone still rang,
but he was not in the other end.
"It seems that he truly loves you," said Lutfiya
when she read his letter.
They have never met
though they are together in the plastic bag.
In my bag of pictures, all my friends are close
to me and to one another
no matter how far they were in real life.

. . .

The garden of the Writers' Union was known as a place
for arguments between writers, especially when they were drunk.
The writers of the '80s argued with the writers of the '70s.
The older generation never wanted to acknowledge
that the younger generation existed.
They said that poetry was ruined by the new poets,
while the new poets said that the work
of their predecessors was obscure and nonsensical.
Poets would come to listen and bring new work
to read. The comments would swing like a pendulum
from those who praised, *Allah, repeat, repeat!*

to those who told you to work on it, or
throw it in the trash. Nssayif Al-Nassiri
would send his praise in a poetic letter.
He said that each new generation abolished the previous one
like the bloody military coups that have ruled Iraq.
Critics referred to my 1980s generation as "the war poets"
and sometimes as "the young poets."
Adnan Al-Saigh was probably the first one to use that title.
The headline of his article was: "Pay attention please,
the 1980s generation is coming."
He interviewed most of us who published during the '80s.

One day, Adnan challenged me to enter
the Hassan Ajmi Coffeehouse with the male poets.
My male friends said that the most important literary discussions
and discoveries occurred in that coffeehouse.
I don't know if any woman had ever entered that place before me,
but after a few minutes of being there, I thought
it was not worth the adventure—
I did not want to discuss poetry or any other issue there.
The tea was not impressive either.
I sat between Adnan and Abdul Razzaq Al-Rubaei.
The men in the coffeehouse, after a minute, ignored me
and turned back to their discussions,
their hookahs, dominos, chessboards, *tasabih* beads,
their dice on the *tawli* boards.
The waiter appeared with ten *istikans* in one hand,
and loudly reminded one of the writers
that he hadn't paid for his tea last time.

One day, I gave Adnan's wife, Majda, a ride home
and absentmindedly took the turn for the Republican Palace
instead of Liberation Square. Two uniformed guards
pointed their rifles at us for so long
that I thought they were trying to take
the best possible aim at their target.
My foot froze on the brake of the car.

Finally one of them approached us, and I thought
he couldn't miss from this distance.
But then he inspected the car and sent
us on our way, saying, "May Allah be with you!"
The words were meaningless to me;
I could not understand what I was hearing.
He had taken my driver's license and jotted some notes
using a pen instead of a rifle,
for according to one of the government's slogans,
"Pens and rifles have one end."

Abdul Razzaq Alrubaei opened his mouth wide with laughter
when he heard how we'd gotten lost at the Republican Palace.
He was easily surprised and laughed suddenly and loudly.
But secretly he was a sad person.
His brother had refused to join the army
and was killed by the government.
His family was not allowed to mourn the death,
and they had to pay for the price of the bullet
that was used to shoot him.

I always complained when Razzaq (as we called him)
gave me a bus ticket. Who knew when the bus would come
or how many people would be crammed inside.
People would hang partly out the door because they couldn't fit inside.
Razzaq said that if he won a million dinars
he would buy a million bus tickets.
We were among the group of "young" poets
who were invited to meet the Minister of Information and Culture,
H. Y. Hammadi, after we were featured in *Asfar* magazine.
He welcomed us saying, "How are the young poets doing?"
but then he said, "This modern poetry doesn't make any sense to me.
Why would someone talk about a turtle when he means to talk about war?
This prose poetry is like marrying a foreign woman."
I had to cover my mouth to stifle my laughter,
and Razzaq passed me a note that said,
"This makes me want to marry a foreign woman."

And he did: in Oman
he married a woman whose mother was British.

Adnan and Razzaq were always together,
sometimes joined by Fadel Khalef Jabr.
One day we left the Young Writers' Club to eat lunch.
Raw meat hung on the walls of the restaurant
and a sickly smell filled the air.
Restaurants would appear and disappear
and be spoken of as legends.

Fadel liked to tell stories about the *maqalib* (practical jokes)
of his friend Jawad Al-Hattab.
Jawad once appeared at Fadel's house after midnight,
saying he was "bored and wanted to go for a walk."
He wouldn't wait for Fadel to change his clothes,
so Jawad stopped a taxi and took Fadel in his pajamas
downtown to Al-Tahrir Square.
Fadel became terrified when he saw some military officers
coming toward them. Officers often wandered around,
and asked every man for their identity card,
searching for those who escaped the war.
They would arrest any man who didn't carry an identity card,
no matter what the excuse. Jawad scared Fadel to death
when he started screaming out,
"My friend isn't carrying an identity card!"
To Fadel's relief, the officers laughed.
I told Fadel, "They probably didn't want to waste their time
with two crazy men, one screaming and one in pajamas."

Ali Abdul Amiir is also in the plastic bag.
We shared a love for Fairouz, the great Lebanese singer.
When the Iraqi newspapers were full of pictures of war,
full of headlines that warned you against
"conspiracies of the enemies and forces of evil,"
you could find an article by Ali about American country music
or rock and roll. Ali once went to

80   ٨.

an Angry Black Shirts' concert
at the Melia Mansour Hotel in Baghdad.
They sang the song "Devil's Paradise" very fast.
The audience, who wore black shirts like the band, started to slam
the chairs on the floor in rhythm to the music.
Hotel management then called the police and stopped the show.
Ali told me that this noise and violence
was a scream of protest against the war.
In the photograph, Ali wears his khaki military uniform and boots.
Years before, his friends called him a "hippie."
He would wear white sneakers and carry a canvas bag
on which he'd written: "Make love, not war."

Another poet of the war generation was Munthir Abdul Hur.
He used to call me "sister."
I remember him always searching for Jan Dammo,
the great absentminded poet.
Jan never held a job. He would
sell his poems to other poets
who had money but lacked inspiration.
The few poems that were left for Jan
were collected into one book: *The Worn Garments*.
During the war with Iran, Jan was enlisted in the army
to serve as a night guard.
He always fell asleep at the wrong times.
Somebody told him: "Jan, you are a soldier.
You can't just sleep whenever you want."
Jan replied: "Why?"
The other one asked: "Why can't you sleep?"
Jan replied: "No, why am I a soldier?"
He was known for his satirical laughter
in response to any traditional or "mobilizing" poem.
We all saw the practices of "the party and revolution" as a joke.
But only Jan actually laughed at the joke.
The rest of us never laughed at the government
except in private with friends that we trusted,
those that wouldn't write secret reports

about you, sending you to hell.
One evening people gathered at the Writers' Union
for Jan's poetry reading but he was nowhere to be found.
Finally he was found at a bar,
and brought to the reading.
Jan read a few lines, then sat down.
He didn't like to read. The hour was filled, instead,
with a talk about him by a few critics.
Jan couldn't care less.
That was Jan's first and last reading.
Always homeless, he was found dead one day
on a street in Australia.

Like Jan Dammo, Yousuf Al-Saigh was closer to young poets
than to the poets of his own generation.
Yousuf was a real poet despite being a senior Baath party member.
He once delayed an important meeting with government officials
to attend one of our poetry readings.
The day I took my manuscript *The Psalms of Absence* to the publisher,
I saw Yousuf by chance on the elevator
at the Ministry of Information and Culture.
The publisher, Al-Adeeb Press,
wanted to include drawings with the poems—
that was the style in those days.
Yousuf—with a long, white beard—looked like Santa Claus.
"Who is doing the drawings?" he asked me.
"I don't know yet," I said.
"Come on, let's take care of that for you," he said, leading me to his office.
He was the director of the Cinema and Theater Department.
"How about Alaa Bashir?" he asked.
"Dr. Alaa Bashir is a great artist but I am sure he's too busy for this," I said.
Dr. Bashir was a famous surgeon and Saddam's personal physician.
People waited months to get an appointment with him.
But Yousuf called him on the phone, and, to my surprise,
the doctor appeared after a few minutes
as he would have for a patient in the emergency room.
Apparently they were close friends

and he might have visited anyway. Dr. Bashir shook my hand.
He was very distinguished, with sharp features like a statue,
bald in the front but long hair in the back.
Yousuf said, "You know this poet, don't you?
I would like you to make sketches of some of her poems.
What do you think?" Dr. Bashir nodded and smiled.
Yousuf handed him some of my poems in a folder
and continued to chat with me about *Rain Man*,
which was being screened at the Cinema Club.
Dr. Bashir started looking through the poems and making sketches
  with a pencil.
I sat there wishing the earth would open up and swallow me.
He had been called to my poems as if to an emergency.
After a short time he put the sketches on the table
and asked us to guess which poems were represented.
Yousuf took the initiative:
"This must be about the woman that has a headache . . .
this one is about the war."
The day I brought Yousuf a copy of my book,
with sketches by Alaa Bashir,
he introduced me to his new wife, pulling back her veil
to show me how he had shaved her bald.
"She must be as crazy as he is," I thought.
His first wife had died in a car accident—
the apples in her car had rolled out with her.
He published a book of poetry about her called
The Lady of the Four Apples.

After *The Psalms of Absence* was published,
I was contacted by Dr. Salah Al-Qassab.
He was known for directing experimental theater.
He told me that his new play was inspired by my poems
and he invited me to attend the opening.
I couldn't associate the scenes with my poetry,
but I was pleased by his enthusiasm.
Most of the scenes involved bathtubs and motorcycles
and characters wearing sunglasses.

One of his students at the Academy of Fine Arts told me
that Dr. Al-Qassab was so obsessed with sunglasses
that he wore them every day. Once, when I was
helping my mother bring the laundry
down from the roof, where the sun had dried and ironed it,
Dr. Al-Qassab arrived with a piano.
The piano had been neglected at the theater, collecting dust and papers.
"I am sure you know its value," he said.
The men could barely move the piano from the truck.
They put it in the corner of our living room, but my mother
didn't like it there. The piano was too heavy to move, though,
so it stayed in the corner, perhaps forever.

. . .

I carried two cups of tea to the garden
where Khalid M. was waiting to interview me.
White *razqi* flowers were in bloom. Khalid
asked me about using chess and geometry in my poetry
and about the wall that collapsed between
our garden and the neighbors'.
I told him how my four brothers and I would sit
in the garden in the evenings, and our neighbors'
daughters would also sit in their garden.
Thank God the wall fell when we were all sleeping.
No one was hurt; the two gardens became one,
and we didn't bother to rebuild as we decided to
share the land. Evenings in the garden sometimes
stretched until midnight, and we even started to share
our appetizers and drinks around the table.

We, being employees of the Ministry of Culture,
were obligated to attend official readings of poetry.
The exits were guarded by policemen, who forced us
to stay the entire time. The poems glorified Saddam
and the army
and had traditional rhyming patterns

and followed the sixteen classical *buhour* (meters/seas)
set out by Al-Khalil Bin Ahmed Al-Farahidi
in the second century of the Hegira.
Sometimes they would read a few *ghazal* poems
as if giving warriors a rest on a march.
Khalid could always find a way to escape.
He could solve any puzzle
even the one of how I was to flee Iraq.
I never thought of poetry as a "profession," but Khalid did.
He convinced the official to write in my passport:
The current profession of the passport bearer is poet.

. . .

I didn't have the chance to read
all the books on my shelves, so I asked
Lutfiya to take some and my cousin
to take the rest, until I could return home
and reclaim them. Banned books
were smuggled into Iraq
wrapped in the covers of approved books.
Hussein Al-Husseini could find you any book
and bring it to you with a laugh. He could
find you cigarettes or get you out of jail.
He was friends with all the ministers
and his pot of Turkish coffee was always hot.
His office still smelled of the pungent beans
when he was taken away to prison. He cursed
everyone there when he was released.
Talking to a director general on the phone, he said,
"How are you, *natoor*?" He used the word *natoor* (guard)
following a speech by Saddam in which he described
government officials as guards. After I left the country,
the government asked my brother to pay
for my university education, which had been free.
I sent him a message to have Al-Husseini accompany him
to the Ministry in case they gave him a hard time.

We were expected to follow directions
and to worry. Only critics could be ignored without concern.
After every war they would present their theories
on postwar literature. But who cares?
There was never a postwar literature in Iraq.

Our 1980s war generation was followed by more war generations.
But it has been said that our generation had a higher number
of women poets than the others, though
still less than the fingers of one hand. Siham Jabbar
was the most modern female poet of our generation
but the most conservative in dress. She wore
the traditional *hijab*, but her parents still
threw her books away hoping she would stop
"wasting her time," help more with the housework,
and get married.

Reem Qais Kuba was the opposite.
She was a modern woman with conservative poetry.
Her parents were gentle, warm, and welcoming.
Their house was like those on Abu Nawas Street.
It overlooked the Tigris River with a big palm tree
in the center of the living room. Women were
forbidden from entering the cafés on Abu Nawas Street
(which smelled deliciously of *masqouf* fish)
without a male chaperone.
So it was a kind of compensation
to be in Reem's backyard looking down at the river
and speaking freely. The river ran between us
and any listening ears.

Another poet, Amal Al-Jibouri, always complained
that we didn't appreciate her. She helped me change
my job through her *wasta* (connections).
After we graduated, Amal accompanied me to the Ministry of Planning
to find my name on the employment bulletin board.
The central employment system of Iraq apparently had decided

that I should teach English. But I had no desire to be a school teacher—
I had planned to be a journalist since childhood.
My parents, on the other hand, expected me
to do something related to mathematics and geometry.
I had always tutored other children in math after school,
but being the worst teacher in the world, I was very impatient
and would never repeat anything more than once.
I didn't care if they copied the answers.
"Don't be mean," my mother would say.
The ministry official Amal knew ordered tea for us. Before we had
even finished our tea, he changed my assignment
from the Ministry of Education to the Ministry of Culture and
Information. I felt as if a judge had found me innocent of a crime
and released me. Amal always complained that I was a chess
master but could not remember the directions to her house.

Sometimes I would get together with Lutfiya al-Dulaimi
when we needed to gossip about other writers
or talk about personal issues
or criticize the government in private.
We would drink fresh mint tea
at five o'clock. She was from a different generation of writers
and would remind me each time we parted
to avoid highways and to read *The Necessity of Art* by Ernst Fischer.
Lutfiya always longed for lovers that were like the characters
in stories she read. "He fills the hotel room with oranges
just to surprise his beloved. She sinks
into the fruit as soon as she enters the room."
She would say, "Life can be beautiful,
don't you think?"
"Life is beautiful if possible," I said.
She believed that only the present moment mattered.
"This moment is the truth," she said. "Now is the time."

But where is the moment?
It vanishes the moment we speak it.
It gives up its space to another moment

and becomes the past. Already the world
lives in the past tense.

Lutfiya cried whenever she thought of her two sons.
They had left and gone to Europe. Half of the people
she knew had left and the other half would leave.
"Who will be left in the city?" she wondered.
"Who will rebuild the beauty that sleeps under the ruins?"
There were writers from the "outside," the media reported,
and writers from the "inside." Eventually all the writers
might flee to the outside to write about the inside from there.

. . .

It was my thirty-first birthday when the plane
carried me to the new land where Columbus
had arrived because the world was round.
I arrived 500 years later because the world was square
and I needed to hide in one of its corners.

The clouds were cotton, as always,
close and far, like a dream.
I decided to pretend that I didn't speak English
to avoid talking to the other passengers.
I didn't want to say I was Iraqi, nor
did it seem appropriate somehow.
What would I say if the woman beside me asked
what I'd be doing in America, why
was I going? But she didn't even speak to me.
She didn't ask about the Gulf War
or even talk about the weather.
She knew her way around the plane
and I imitated her, pressing the same buttons on or around the seat.
We were in first class, which was a mistake. In Amsterdam,
the airline scared me when they said I didn't have a ticket
to America, only one from Amman to Amsterdam.
I explained that I had paid for a full ticket through to America,

that I knew no one in Amsterdam, that I had nowhere else to go.
So they gave me the only seat left on the flight,
which was in first class. Of course, I didn't mind.
These businessmen and women
had never been to the Mredi Souq in Baghdad,
where you can buy back your stolen goods
at double the price! I was an important person
on that plane, greeted and smiled at,
watching a tiny television, eating pistachios
and drinking red wine.
None of these things were meant for me.

I accidentally spilled wine on my shirt
and remembered my mother,
who sorted all spilled things into good and bad:
spilt sugar brings good luck; spilt
salt brings bad luck. If you drop
a dish, it depends:
if it breaks, good; if not, bad.
Coffee depends if it is sweet or bitter.
I couldn't remember her rules about wine.

I was frightened by sudden turbulence on the plane,
but the people in first class kept reading or sleeping.
I imitated them and set my fears aside.
I had spent nine months in Amman. After that,
even a baby is ready to be born. I edited the poems
I had written in Jordan. Each poem started with one
particular Arabic letter. I couldn't remember
why I had written them that way.

We descended to Detroit
and the stewardess wished me a good day.
It was not a matter of one day, I wanted to reply.

At customs I was escorted aside.
An official asked me questions

and flipped suspiciously through my passport.
She couldn't believe I had gotten a tourist visa
from beneath the ruins. They took my fingerprints
many times, and photographs of me.
I was not sure if I was supposed to smile.
Was I a famous poet or a criminal?

The official stamped my passport
and another mistake was made.
She stamped it May 1997 instead of May 1996,
giving me a year and three months
instead of three months. Maybe she liked
my fingerprints, which can be traced
to pencils and tears. One day my fingers
will cover the eyes of my friends
in Iraq again, and I will ask my friends
to guess who is behind them.
In baggage claim my suitcase revolved alone,
as confused as I was.

Lori was my immigration lawyer.
She was the first American to join
my plastic bag of photographs.
It was she who noticed the mistake on my visa.
I could have added Mazin's name to my asylum application
if he were still alive. I looked for his name
on a list of prisoners of war but it was not there
or on any other list. To be alive, a trace
must remain. I had no trace of him—
only the photograph from the University of Baghdad,
which was fading. The trace of his hand on mine
could not be produced or eliminated.

It was Lori who showed me the Statue of Liberty.
She also took me to the place
where the Twin Towers used to stand.
I imagined those people

with their interrupted conversations
in the middle of their lives.

I told Lori about the Censorship Department in Iraq
that protected "public morals" by cutting away
anything "inappropriate." You were required to submit
your book to them before it could be published.
But their approval didn't protect you from trouble.
They think of themselves as training another censor:
you. The sudden disappearance of other writers
is supposed to train you.
When the censors read my book, *Diary of a Wave Outside the Sea*,
one of them asked: "Who is this god, Zeus, in your poem?"
"It is not the writer's job to explain," I told him.
"It is the reader's task to understand."

Once the Camal Press in Germany sent me three banned books.
Two men appeared in my boss's office at the *Baghdad Observer*.
They asked me if I had ordered these books.
"No," I said.
"Do you want these books?" one of them asked me.
"No," I answered. Eventually they left with the books
and without me! My boss, N. Al-Hadithi, a gentle man,
seemed relieved. He eventually
became the Minister of Foreign Affairs.
As the Director General, he never had a mustache,
but as the Minister he had a mustache.
Saddam had ordered all government officials
to grow mustaches and to lose weight.

In our cozy old building, Dar Al-Jamahir,
we would place our finished articles in a reed basket
that hung from a long rope, and dangle
the basket down to the floor below
so the editors could type, cut, and paste the articles,
and find photographs to go with the stories.
Our newspaper was laid out like all Iraqi newspapers:

on the front page, the president's picture and his activities
with a reminder in the corner to "write with no fear
or hesitation whether the government liked it or not."
This was just for decoration.
On the third floor was the cafeteria,
where we could go at any time and talk about anything
but politics. Once I asked about a colleague,
Hassan Mutalq, who had once signed his novel for me
with some words about chess. They whispered
that he had disappeared. "Don't ask," they said.

Our articles could either be handwritten or typed.
Mine were usually covered with arrow-corrections
and curved lines. You would not find that in Huda's articles.
She would retype the whole thing each time
she made an error. Reuters' English didn't need correction
except when it disagreed with Our Wise Government.
So the "invasion" of Kuwait became the "annexation" of Kuwait.
Sometimes I was absentminded about these kinds of corrections.
But the managing editor, whom we called Abo Iman, would
always catch my mistakes. Someone asked him if he,
as a Kurd, supported Talabani or Barazani.
"I support Tarazani," he said. He justified changing
the Associated Press English from American
into British English with this joke:
An American and a British man are arguing.
The American says, "We invented elevators,
so that gives us the right to name them."
The Brit replies, "We invented English
so that gives us the right to name them."

Sometimes Huda and I would walk to the River Street market
together to tell each other secrets. The two other female journalists
at the *Baghdad Observer*, Esra and Ban, would occasionally
join us and tell interesting stories,
like the one about the Abbas lock for wishes.
You must return and unlock your wishes

if you want them to come true. For one woman
forgot to unlock her wishes until it was too late
and her true love married his cousin.

. . .

Lori stapled an article from an Iraqi newspaper
to my asylum papers that listed me, with other writers,
as a "traitor" and "America" as my country of residence.
I first wanted to go to America in 1983
for very different reasons. I always excelled at math
and my father wanted to send me to America
to get a good education at his expense so I could
"introduce the world to my mathematical inventions."
My uncle, who lived in Detroit, sent me
an admission packet for Wayne State University.
I was required to take an English language course there first,
which with room and board cost $11,000 a year. "That's no problem,"
my father said. "The Iraqi dinar equals three American dollars."

I told everyone I was going to study abroad.
I talked about it twelve hours a day
and spent the other twelve dreaming out the details:
how I would live independently in an apartment,
read whatever I wanted (including all the banned books).
I would invite only a few guests to my place,
and live without arranged marriages.
I would escape from the pettiness
through isolation with books
thousands of miles away from war
and sirens
and explosions.
I would live far away from the trashy
propaganda literature
the Iraqi and Iranian missiles
perpetually aimed at each other,
far away from the two tv channels and

the signs on the street that read "Every Iraqi
is a Martyrdom Project"
and "All Iraqis Are Baathists—
Even Those Who Don't Belong."
Away, away from all that broken glass
between the colorful wings
in a caterpillar's dream.

I remember riding the swings in the garden
with the girl next door the day before
I was to go to the Ministry of Foreign Affairs
to pick up my travel papers.
My mother said, "People in America are crazy.
They raise cats and dogs in their homes."

It all came to nothing.
The current law prohibits Iraqi women
from studying abroad at their own expense
during the war. My father said it was
an exceptional law for an exceptional time
and that it would probably be changed
after the war. He suggested I study English
literature at Baghdad University, to prepare
myself when the law changed.

. . .

In the open courtyard at the College of Arts
we argued about Shakespeare
and ate chickpeas from the street vendors.
Sometimes we walked to the British Council
to borrow English books and movies,
and to drink tea and coffee in their fantastic garden
where couples reclined under the shady trees.

With the books, movies, and lecture notes under our arms,
we went to demonstrations. We were told to

"Implement, then ask." The demonstrations
turned into opportunities. We would discuss
art and literature: the plays of Awni Karomi
the music of Naseer Shamma
the paintings and red socks of Sattar Kawoosh.
No one paid attention to the student leaders
who screamed at the front of the pack.

I was busy
and America slipped from my mind.
The Wayne State application was forgotten in a drawer
with some poems that I wouldn't dare publish
and a notebook from elementary school
filled with colorful drawings.

When I graduated, the law had not changed:
I still could not go to America.
Then Ghada, a deaf painter, invited me
to accompany her to America as her translator.
We used to communicate through her notebook,
or her low, slow mumblings. Once,
I invited her to a poetry reading of mine
only remembering afterward that she
wasn't able to hear a thing. She sat
smiling in silence. Ghada had once painted
the Minister of Defense and gave him the painting
as a present. In return, he decided to pay for her treatment
abroad. And I had filled her notebooks with criticisms of Iraqi war
literature, of writing filled with disgusting heroism and Iraqi soldiers
as supermen, of "medals of courage" given daily
to generals and killers, of awards given to
writers who praise the killing.
I wanted to ask her not to show him the notebook,
but I didn't. She said, "He's a son of a bitch.
I had to paint him." Then she invited me to be her translator
because the *makrama* (personal gift) included a companion.

At the passport office I wrote in her notebook:
"A family member, not a stranger, is preferable as a companion,
unless no family members are capable." But no one
in her family spoke or read English. So we brought letters
to support this. After my passport was issued, I asked them,
"I thought the law prohibits Iraqi women from traveling abroad
during wartime?" They explained that women are
permitted to travel when they are sent by the government.

On the airplane, Ghada wrote in her notebook
that the first thing she wanted to do was see the Statue of Liberty.
"We are going to San Francisco, not New York," I wrote back.

We walked across the Golden Gate Bridge
and took pictures of the pigeons. I had never seen pigeons
walking fearlessly on the ground before. Ghada
wanted to watch a movie on tv but I kept
changing the channels to see how many there were.
Ghada had lost her hearing at age fourteen
when she caught typhoid fever. "What I miss most
is listening to Um Kulthum sing," she wrote.

The hospital was so clean, not one cricket.
The doctors told her she needed surgery
to implant a hearing device. She said
she would think about it,
but she was too scared of the surgery
and never returned to the hospital.

At Disneyland, Ghada asked me if I would return to Iraq
or stay in America. I think she was afraid of
what would happen if she returned without me.
But I missed my home, family, friends,
and Mazin's face, welcoming me back
on Wednesday at the Writers' Union.

. . .

After I graduated, my father's kidneys failed.
It was the first time in his life that he had to go to a hospital.
The doctors told him that only Ibn Al-Bitar Hospital
could treat his illness properly. But we needed
approval from the Ministry of Health for his transfer.
We visited one office after another
one department after another
one ministry after another
one *wasta* after another.
My father was not a member of the Baath party
and possessed no military rank.
His *wasta* was Abo Faisal, his friend
who co-owned a hotel with him.
Abo Faisal returned from vacation
just to help with my father's situation.

"Come back tomorrow," they say,
anytime you need a paper from a government office.
"My father is in critical condition," I told them. "Can't you
please give me the transfer today?"
"This is impossible . . ."
"Papers must be signed . . ."
"I will do my best as soon as I receive them . . ."

My father lay sadly in bed.
He had not slept the night before
because the girl beside him had screamed
all night for her mother. When he finally fell asleep,
he woke up a short time later to find her gone,
and didn't know if she had been moved
or had died. He was trying not to cry.
I never saw my father cry.
When his mother died, he stepped outside
and lit a cigarette. It was the only time I saw
him smoke. His cigarettes were only for guests.

My grandmother forgot everything before she died

except her childhood home. Toward the end
she would gather her clothes in a big sheet, tie it,
and try to open the door in the middle of the night
because she wanted to go to her "father's home"
(as she called it). She forgot the names of people
and who they were. She forgot that her brother died
a few minutes after giving her condolences.
She would walk in her sleep and my mother
was afraid she'd walk right off the roof.
It was the same roof we slept on during
the summers, where years ago my grandmother
used to tell me bedtime stories. Later I realized
these stories were folktales known in many cultures.
As a child I was eager to hear them over and over again,
and always asked her whether the tales were in any book.
I yearned to see the pictures of the stories
and read every detail myself. She repeated the same answer,
"I wish they were in a book to give you.
I learned them from my grandmother.
And you will teach them the same way
to your grandchildren."
No one was surprised when she died.
At the last moment she pointed to the ceiling
and said she saw two birds.
My mother wondered if they were birds
or angels descending to carry her away to paradise.

My father loved to tell me stories during naptime.
His favorite was the story of two brothers Ajiib and Ghariib.
They were separated as children and followed two different paths.
Sometimes they would cross paths without knowing it.
Each day he would tell me part of the story, and then
fall asleep snoring despite the excitement of the tale.
I would try to wake him in vain, opening his eyes with my fingers.

I left his hospital room to find a nurse
and bumped into three people in white coats.

One was a doctor and two were students
who were learning from my father's case.
The doctor said, "I must tell you
that his condition is critical."

We still did not have the approval papers
for the transfer to Ibn Al-Bitar.
Tomorrow, tomorrow. . .

"It is in Allah's hands," they told me at the Ministry.
"Be glad that you will get it eventually.
Some people do not even have that."

I returned to the hospital but visiting hours were over.
I rushed into the elevator and the receptionist chased me
and my brother chased him. I pressed the CLOSE button
right in the receptionist's face.
Upstairs the doctor was pressing on my father's heart.
A red cricket was perched near his foot—
I slapped it away. The doctor turned to me in pity.
In the reception area, I spotted my youngest brother,
who was in first grade, sitting apart from the rest
of the family, looking out the window.
I looked at my mother, with no words.
She immediately knew. She cried in our Aramaic dialect,
"Your father is gone, gone, gone . . ."

My father was wheeled away,
and when I asked where he was going,
they said the dead were stored in the freezer
until they were buried.
We sat in the parking lot and cried
as much as we wanted to.

At home, everyone wore black.
My aunt had hired a woman
who sang and chanted for the dead.

Her poetry was sad but not very good.
She sang about my mother as a widow.
Our house was full of people.
The men smoked
while the women cried and wailed,
slapping their chests and chanting
the names of their martyrs.

On the fourth day, my youngest brother wanted to watch cartoons,
but my aunt objected and said that he should be ashamed.
My mother had no say in the matter. Relatives
were always interfering with our lives. They said
that our father's death had broken our backs.
It was true something inside us had broken,
but I didn't want them to see our vulnerability.

My father returned to me in my dreams,
hiding something behind his back
as he did when I was a little girl, or telling me
he wasn't dead when they put him in the freezer.
In most of my dreams he was silent.

Shortly after my father died, the war ended.
People fired their guns into the sky.
The bullets were not aimed at anyone for a change
but would descend randomly to earth.
That was 8-8-88.
The war had lasted eight years.
The number 8 was supposed to be lucky.
Everyone was full of joy
celebrating in the streets and on top of cars;
loud music blared everywhere
and the hotels were quickly busy again booking weddings.
But the black signs of the martyrs
still covered the city walls.

My father never lived to see peace. He died

worrying about my brothers, worrying they would
graduate before the end of the war and be sent off
to the front lines. I wished he could have seen
that they were fine.

I had never seen my mother so worried,
she who always left everything to God.
During the war, a missile hit a silo near my college.
She and my father waited for me at our front door
and were so relieved when they saw I wasn't injured.
"I told you, the Virgin Mary always protects our kids,"
she told my father, "Every time you
do something good for other people,
God will save you from one more danger
and you may never even know it."

After my father's death, my mother started waiting for us
at the front door. I had never heard her talk about
the dangers of the world before except those that God
eliminated in exchange for good deeds. Now,
she started to tell us, "Be careful. Never interfere
in politics. Never criticize the government."
She spoke about young men and women
who disappeared, never to be seen again.
She began locking our doors, though she
never locked them when my father was alive.
One time she even chastised me for locking our door:
Guests were always dropping by and she yelled,
"What a shame! Do you want our guests to knock?"
Even after my father's death
the chai pot was always hot,
smelling of cardamom and shaking
and clattering, as if it too
were part of the conversation and the company.

. . .

One day a classmate approached me and said,
"It's a shame you are not a Baath party member.
A good person like you should definitely join."
I had to tell her that it was hard for me to attend the meetings
but that I would think about it.

Before the Gulf War, my mother was pouring
a second round of tea for our guests
when one family friend said that Saddam
had already gotten approval to annex Kuwait.
Others said there would be no war
because Saddam would withdraw the troops at the last moment,
giving America no excuse to attack.
Still others said there would be war:
the price of food was already going up,
as if the merchants longed for war prices.
People spoke endlessly of war.

I hated waking up early,
but on January 17, 1991,
my mother woke me at 2 a.m.
War had arrived again.
I wished just this once
it had let us sleep in.

My mother screamed at me
to join her and my four brothers.
She had made a special room, sealing
the windows and covering the keyhole with tape
to keep out chemical weapons.
We couldn't even use the bathroom after the sirens started;
she said we would live or die, together, in that spot.
That was the rule.
The explosions always seemed
to be getting progressively louder and closer.

My mother prayed:

"God, who is full of mercy, will save us."
I thought of Yehuda Amichai
who wrote that if not for God-full-of-mercy,
there would be mercy in the world
and not just in Him.

We took turns trying to light a candle
but none of us succeeded.
We were suffocating in that sealed-up room, without
oxygen. The telephone rang, distantly.
Strangely enough, the electricity and telephone
were still working. During the previous war,
the lights had blinked on and off
every time the sirens wailed.
Over the phone, our relatives said
that if we had gasoline
we should all flee to Telkaif—they had heard
the Americans would not strike there.
My mother spoke to them
until the phone finally went dead in her hand.

My Aunt Dura lived in the village of our ancestors.
Cows, chickens, and donkeys filled
most of the space, crowding
us into one room.
How lucky for the animals!
They were not at war.
But who knows, perhaps they, too,
were frightened and disturbed
by the planes zooming overhead
and the distant explosions in the middle of the night.

We would sit in a circle around the radio
and listen to the news. When commercials
came on between broadcasts
we would turn the radio off to save the batteries.
My cousin once appeared, carrying a sack of flour,

and said, "We will be completely cut off if the batteries die,
and these days batteries cost as much as a wedding."
My aunt went through that flour in one week, feeding us.
Her face was always red from baking in the clay *tanoor*.
The only thing she ever said about politics was,
"I don't think Bush will attack Telkaif
because so many Chaldeans have relatives in America."

At night, we froze.
There was no gas for the heater.
We would have been even colder
if the room hadn't been so crowded with people.
Nobody dared mention a shower.
My aunt put a bucket outside to catch the rain,
but the water it collected was black.

The radio said that power stations in Baghdad
had been attacked. This reminded my mother
that she had filled our freezer with food for wartime.
It upset her to imagine the food rotting.
She kept repeating, "How could we forget
to bring all that food? Why did we leave
in such a hurry and bring nothing?"

After ten days, we decided to return to Baghdad
despite the news that it was still being heavily bombed.
"Are you crazy?" my cousin asked.
"You may return to find your home gone.
Here you can only hear the sound of the airplanes,
but there you will hear sirens and explosions day and night."

The first thing we noticed was the wide crack in the wall
between our garden and our neighbor's garden.
The wall that we never bothered to fix, even after the war,
when the wall suddenly fell down.

At home, I enjoyed the luxury of smelling our *razqi* flowers

though bullets were scattered on the grass.
I enjoyed taking showers
(though I had to count the drops)
and lying in bed reading my books.
The floor under my bed shook from the explosions,
and my reading was interrupted by the sirens,
but my mother let us sleep in our own beds:
home sweet home.

As we drank our tea, my mother expressed her astonishment
that the Americans (whom she had always seen as
good, Christian people) caused her to throw away
all the food she had frozen after spending so much time making it.
We had never eaten canned food before—my mother
was too proud of her complicated cooking and enjoyed it too much.
She would wake early to prepare everything,
measuring and mixing and adding spices very seriously
and in such large quantities that it always seemed
there was a campaign being organized in the kitchen.
Everyone in the neighborhood—friends and relatives—
knew her for this. But the "mother of all battles"
introduced us to canned food.
We enjoyed the food, despite the cans
and despite (or because of) the small quantities.
We didn't want to run out of cans before the war ended
because our car was out of gas
and only Ammo's store was within walking distance,
and it was closed. He had used his cans
to feed his family—his wife, his three sons, their wives
and children, and his parents all lived with him.
After forty days, a ceasefire was announced.
Iraqi soldiers were recalled from Kuwait.
Some were barefoot
and killed by Allied troops as they returned home.
Employees were recalled to their jobs.
A reconstruction campaign was announced.

On our way to work, we avoided the bridges
that had been destroyed.
We couldn't make any phone calls
since the communications system had been bombed.
We had electricity, but only for a few hours a day.
Birds couldn't even find wires to perch on.
UN sanctions were still imposed, shrinking
everything into smaller and smaller sizes,
whether it was bread or books.
Because of this acute shortage of paper,
my cousin ripped up the books he was keeping for me
and used the paper to wrap falafel he sold in his store.

Abdul Amir Jaras sent me his new book of poetry
that was the size of a book of matches.
I wrote some new war poems,
this time using both sides of the page.
My mother sat barefoot on the floor
and read my poem "Pronouns,"
which had been published that day in the newspaper.
It was the first time I saw her read one of my poems
and I was nervous.
"He plays a train, she plays a whistle, they move away,"
she read aloud.
"I think children will like this poetry."
"Why children?" I asked.
"Isn't this written for children?" she asked.
"I'm not sure," I said.

She told me how proud she was of me
and how, when I was born,
my aunts cried because I was a girl.
They thought that their brother was too good for a daughter.
But their sadness lasted for only two years,
until my oldest brother was born.
They greeted him with cheers and *halahils*
but no one in the hospital told them about his mental disability.

I left my mother and went into my room.
There I wrote:

My mother gives birth to a girl
while everyone waits for a boy.
They receive the child with frowns
but she cannot go back where she came from.
She arches her back and lets out her first cry.

Her mother gives her a pencil and notebook
to keep her busy
and she draws herself as a flower.
A lover passes by
and picks her for his beloved.
The lovers talk about drying her
and pressing her between the pages of a book.
They walk side by side.
The flower thinks:
How will I bear the eternal dryness?

The girl turns the page in her notebook
and draws herself as a clock.
She ticks for others
and trembles on certain days.
Some need her to ring early in the morning
some would throw her away
if she did not tell the right time.
Every day at midnight
the hands embrace and forget about the world.

The girl turns the page again
and draws herself as a treasure
in somebody's dream.
She disappears when he wakes up.
She draws herself as a blot
in the history books
beside all the other blots.

She is frightened of the eraser
that wipes the pages clean.

She draws herself as a tree
tickled by a bird perched in her branches.
She laughs and her fruit falls down.
People pass under her leaves.
One scratches two names on her trunk
with Cupid's arrow.
Another takes an ax to her.
That cage, over there
was her body
and the bird inside it
seems familiar to her.

The girl turns the page
and draws herself as a sun.
She divides her time equally between people
but never rests.
She draws herself as an eraser
and goes through all the pages of the notebook.
She returns it to her mother
as clean as it was in the beginning.
She has one wish:
not to be drawn as a boy
and be taken to the front.

. . .

Every day I thanked God for making me a girl—
I didn't want to be called to military service
I didn't want to show my identity card in the street
I didn't want to have to kill anyone—
I could simply lie in my bed
and listen to music
instead of generals who were strict and without mercy
as Mazin said.

I didn't receive any letters from Mazin, though the second
war had ended, too. Did he know that I had changed my address?
At the Baghdad post office, the mailman told me that I was spoiled,
asking for letters to be forwarded to a new address.
"You should notify the senders of your new address yourself," he said.

The long absence of Mazin worried me
and the long absence of my father
worried my mother.
She wandered back and forth between the door
and the kitchen table, or sat staring at me.

One day I attended a strange meeting
in the Sahat Al-Ihtifalat theater, the "Courtyard of Celebrations."
It was compulsory for every journalist to attend
and meet with Uday, Saddam's eldest son.
There were rumors of a *makrama* for the journalists.
So we sat and waited. On the stage in front of us,
two men sat silently. One was the editor-in-chief
of *Al-Qadissiya* and the other was the editor-in-chief
of *Al-Jumhouriya*—two local newspapers
run by the government (though all newspapers
in Iraq were run by the government).
The third chair was empty, waiting for Uday.
After a few hours of doing nothing we watched a frowning, slim man
walk onstage and sit in the empty chair.
He read from a paper in his hand:
"Uday sends you greetings and conveys to you this letter."
The letter was a long lecture on national morals and citizenship
and concluded by saying that the two men sitting in front of us
had betrayed our *watan*, our homeland.
Then someone in the front row
threw garbage at the two editors,
and two armed men appeared
and escorted the editors away
leaving the red, elegant stage empty
and us with our anonymous, silent cowardice.

I wandered around the parking lot, unable to find my car.
I couldn't remember where I had parked
and I watched the faces disperse—
yellow faces, sprouting the horns of sheep.

I wandered in a silent demonstration by myself,
and wondered who brought garbage to the theater,
a theater that was meant for a different kind of performance.
Shakespeare's plays are also full of violence,
but when the show is over the actors appear as themselves
and bow to the audience, the killers
holding hands with the killed.
This play reminded me more of an ugly local tale
of a groom who killed a cat in front of his bride
so that she would fear and obey him for the rest of their lives.

I drove home and went straight to bed.
The next day I didn't get up for work.
"Are you sick?" my mother asked.
"No, but I am going to quit."
She questioned me until I told her what had happened.
She reminded me that employees could not quit
without a *mumala*, or written permission.
I would also have to pay back my college tuition.
After a week, Huda called
and told me that she had submitted sick leave for me
but that it was ending.
I returned to work
waiving my intention to protest, waiving
my entire homeland.
I was in a false exile
and I longed to be in a real one.

I decided to flee the country
though I had no time to say good-bye.
My brother's wedding was in two weeks.
"I think you should leave immediately," he told me.

"Your life is more important than my party.
We'll send you a video later."

Lutfiya said, "I told you publishing that poem
about Zeus was risky. You knew it and just ignored me.
Did you think they have hearts? No.
They would hurt anyone and not think twice about it."

. . .

Outside Iraq, I often dream of returning home.
Sometimes I am regretful, or frustrated,
or afraid of being trapped.
Sometimes I am eager
to surprise my friends with my return.
Other dreams I can't remember.

The alarm clock wakes me early in the morning for work.
The red, yellow, and brown leaves of Michigan's fall
crunch under the feet of children on their way to school.
I have to arrive before them.
I have to be prepared, ready the classroom,
receive them at the door.
Most of them have Arab backgrounds
and they know how to speak Arabic
but cannot read or write it. We open
the textbook from right to left
and some of them say,
"This is a backward language."

The classroom is always a chaotic
din of loud voices where rules are broken
and erasers leave marks on papers.
I don't know how to be strict with teenagers.
My classroom looks like an invaded country.

Louise was a bilingual education supervisor.

We met when I was working at a Border's bookstore
and she asked if I'd be interested in being a bilingual teacher's aid.
I didn't hesitate to leave my job, but when I began
helping in a classroom, I felt as if my interpretations
were constantly interrupting the teacher.
I longed for a classroom of my own. Then,
when I was finally given one, I was constantly
interrupted by my own students.

Louise had six cats. I met only five of them
as one was too shy to meet strangers.
Louise is in my bag of pictures
picking raspberries from a bush in her backyard.

My acceptance letter from Wayne State University
had expired. I was fifteen years late.
They let me apply again, and when I began my classes
it was completely unlike Baghdad University.
I didn't know any other students by name.
We didn't chat after class, eat chickpeas from vendors,
go on trips to the lunar park,
wear white, gray, and blue uniforms,
or march in demonstrations.
The windows never shook from missiles
as they had shaken continuously in Baghdad.
And Mazin wasn't there.

But my telepathy worked.
His letter found me. It had wandered
around the world for ten years,
but at last it arrived, and had not expired.

Like the fish that had once swallowed my ring,
his letter was opened carefully
to reveal its contents.

He had been sending letters to my old address in Iraq.

Then, one day, he saw my poem "The Exodus of Friends"
in a London-based Arabic newspaper.
He contacted the paper and asked for my address.
Like a message in a bottle thrown into the sea
his letter traveled from continent to continent,
hand to hand, until at last it reached Huda in Iraq.
She forwarded it to Michigan
where it finally reached me
all the way from Australia
with a stamp of a kangaroo.

Mazin flew to Detroit.
In the airport he hugged me.
He looked so much older—
his hair was gray and he was balding.
My hair was the same—I had dyed it.
"I couldn't believe it when I finally heard from you," he said.
"I couldn't believe you weren't married.
You are too old to still be single," he added.
"You, too!" I replied.
"I read your letter ten times," he said.
"Me, too!" I replied.
Our reunion was on April Fool's Day.
Mazin's visa was only good for three months.
No one made a mistake with his visa.
Because we weren't married
before I filed for asylum, he couldn't stay
in the U.S. legally until I was a citizen
and we married then. I wouldn't be
a citizen for another ten years! They wanted us to
wait ten years. They didn't care about our
previous ten years we had already lost.

Then Lori told me about an exceptional
residency visa. "Try applying for it," she said.
"You're a distinguished poet—
hopefully they'll realize that."

I sent in the application
with a thick attachment of my literary archive.
My papers had always been messy and scattered
but I made everything neat and orderly.
They sent back a denial, saying I had to have a Nobel Prize
or some equivalent. We laughed at that.
"A Nobel Prize would be too late," I said.

My arrival to America was delayed by twelve years,
my study at Wayne State by fifteen years,
my marriage by ten years.
I couldn't afford any more delays.
I wished I could leave the state of laws
and return to the state of no laws again—
but only for a moment.
There was no *wasta* here to help me along.
I missed my friends in Iraq
who would have lit one last match,
the last match in the box.
Then the box would be as empty as a grave
denied by the dead . . . but that light!

. . .

We continued our absence
in colors and pictures
rolling our song along blindly
like a rushing wheel.
We knew that Aladdin's lamp
was extinguished in our hands,
but we still tried to throw our light
over the land, over the places that
held our hopes, our dreams, our childhoods.
We endeavored to save each other
but were too helpless to save the world.
And now, older, we just wanted the world
to leave us alone.

I found a new soap with a wonderful refreshing scent,
but it still couldn't wash away the smell of gunpowder.

I am sorry I left you among the ruins.
I am sorry I left without saying good-bye.
I apologize to my new home, for carrying the ruins with me.
I apologize for not being able to be in two places at once.
I apologize to the war for avoiding its nightmares
by turning my face to the wall.
I apologize to the sirens
for preferring the sound of music
and the rhythm of water fountains.
I apologize for running to lose weight
instead of running to escape explosions.
I have left my friends, too
busy for their sufferings.
Life continues behind their backs.
I am sorry. Away from you,
I look at the blue spaces between skyscrapers
in the America of lottery tickets,
credit cards, and fast food.
I leave you
and I love you.

The world blinked on and off for us like Christmas lights,
linking us somehow, on and off,
and we were astonished.
Our dreams turned tirelessly
like the pages of a calendar.
We grew old
but our dead and our memories do not age.
Poetry touches us so we burn
for life and despite life.

I was a fish before I was human
and sometimes I long for that life
unfettered in the sea.

Sometimes I suffocate on the land.

Now I prefer e-mail to letters.
A world run by a mouse
where everything can be done
or undone in an instant,
where everything, even
Iraq, still exists
and can never be deleted
not even by accident.
It is saved somewhere in duplicate copies
enlarged or reduced
in pictures and icons, ideas, events,
people. Pandora's box, unopened.
Inside the box: friends carrying used books on Al-Mutanabi Street,
the smells of *masqouf* fish and tea with cardamom
boiling like familiar dust.
On another shore, the rabbit and the turtle stop racing.
They suddenly realize that the race was never the point.

I move the mouse to click on my collection
of poetical numbers.
I like the numerical codes
I found in America:
143 for I love you
187 for I'll kill you
143-2-187 for I love you to death.
Even in the midst of technology
people always need emotion.
Words have their secret lives, vivid
and mercurial, far away
from sheets of paper.
They have consecutive deaths
and great forgetfulness. They are nomads
who don't know why they emigrate
or why they stay behind.
They expand or shrink, always flexible

and ready to give up their nouns and verbs to satisfy us.
They return at the slightest thought.
The word "exile," for example, shifts through various colors and meanings
and the exile yearns with every drift.

I move the mouse to the icon of dancing.
Rhythm liberates us from censorship.
Dancing sends wavy beats
and the beats wake up the universe.
The uninterrupted movement of the universe
causes the phenomenon of multiple dimensions,
and we dance that universal dance when we write.
If we are self-censors, the dance is ruined.
When we sleep, the ghosts dance.
Perhaps they fight, get drunk, and curse one another
as they struggle for existence.
We never know. We are busy gods:
watching television, reading the newspaper,
feeling grateful for the many things
that don't happen to us.

These tales pop up when I click the mouse:

The Frog and the King
There once was a frog who hopped
in the mind of a king. With every hop,
a war broke out. The people were puzzled.
They couldn't figure out how to stop the frog from hopping.
As the number of widows and orphans grew out of control
meetings were held to try to convince the frog
not to hop, or at least to hop
somewhere else, away from the king's mind.
"Poor king," they said, "it is not his fault . . ."

Moon Talk
The moon in the sky
spoke to the moon in the river.

The first moon was lonely
and asked the second moon
to climb into the sky.
"I don't have anyone to tell my secrets to," he said.
"The universe is too busy.
I overlook everything
without getting involved.
I need a friend."
The moon in the river did not reply.
At last the first moon said, "Fine, I will come down
since you cannot come up.
Anyway, it is always easier
to fall than to rise."
So the moon jumped into the river
and was swept away in the gushing current.
Only in the darkness did it discover the truth.

The Volleyball
The volleyball bounced among the hands of the players.
The players threw it, or caught it, or hit it away.
The volleyball was afraid of the hands,
but rebounded back and forth helplessly
waiting to fall to the ground
as if into the arms of a lover.
A little boy seized the ball and put her away
between four walls.
She didn't complain;
she dreamed of a world
on the other side of the walls.

The Mirror
All the pictures we have lived
are behind us in the mirror,
on the other side of the glass.
Weddings, wars, sex,
crimes, laughter, wrinkles.
The mirror is there to receive each scene.

It doesn't know that one crack
would be enough to shatter everything.

The Old Land
Once upon a time,
the new land marched to the old land
and said, "Look, I came to save you.
You need new blood."
The old land said, "O, but I am already full of blood.
You see, there is blood everywhere:
in the rivers
on the sand
under the buildings
in the houses
in the hospitals."
"I mean you need a renewal," the new land said.
"Therefore I am sending you
my young sons and daughters. They will
cross the seas and the deserts to reach you.
We will wake you from your slumber
to give you this present."
"A present?" the old land asked. "I live only in the past."
"A present means a gift," the new land said,
"It is something called Democracy."
"So far," the old land said, "I have seen only the promise of it."
The new land scolded, "You didn't know how to receive it.
You ruined it."
"I am used to ruins," the old land said.
"I am always making more of them."

. . .

The heart of a loved one is always concealed
under layers of skin. We need
a fortune-teller to say:
the war will end, your lover will return,
your sadness will recede,

the sun will not be absent
too much longer, presidents
will transform into sweet, wise people
who hesitate before launching an attack.
If only there was a charm
to protect little hands
from the big ones that hold weapons.

I thought my wedding to Mazin
would be a magical event.
Instead, my dress was so long
I could hardly walk in it; the reception
was boring and the band was bad.
Everything was picked in a hurry
and criticized by our relatives.
The wedding was badly organized.
Everyone left early
because it was a Wednesday and not a weekend.
But Lori came, directly from the airport,
and Louise with her husband, Jim,
who brought a pair of white doves
and set them free. It was beautiful
to see the doves fly away—back home.
Our marriage caused problems with immigration
but resulted in our daughter:
Larsa. Larsa was an ancient Mesopotamian city
and the goddess of the sun.

. . .

America is but a baby of a country.
She doesn't really mean to cause problems.
She always thinks it's easier to replace problems
than to fix them. "Your washer is broken,"
the repairman says. "It is easier to replace it than to fix it."
"Your country is broken," the politician says.
"It is easier to replace it than to fix it."

America bombs with one hand
and shelters with the other.
It used to be hard for people in my big, new country
to find my small, old one on the map.
But the war made it popular.
It is often featured on the front page
of the newspaper like a Hollywood star.
Americans use positive phrases
even in the worst situations.
It is easy to be optimistic when you are young.

Bush the son followed in his father's footsteps
and started his presidency with a war on Iraq.
The father and the son and Clinton
was the holy spirit. His attack on Iraq
was small in comparison.

Saddam and Bush both promised victory.
Sanctions are lifted, but Iraqis don't care.
They stand in long lines
for gasoline either way. They
get their fingers painted when they go to vote
and say: "All the politicians are puppets,
but they are better than Saddam."
In the morning the new ministers go to work,
and in the afternoon they go to religious marches
and strike their faces in mourning.

Now the censors don't have offices:
they have guns. Children sell melted ice
and adults sell children.
The prisoners escape their cells
—innocent and criminals alike—
to mingle with the garbage that fills the streets.
Thieves steal animals from the zoo.
The animals cannot cause
any more destruction running loose

than what has already been caused by humans.
Masked men with swords stand behind kidnapped hostages.
American soldiers learn a few phrases of the Iraqi dialect:
Food.
Danger.
Put your hands up!
Put your hands down.
Talk more slowly.
Don't talk.
Lay down.
Where are you wounded?
Whose fault is it?

Abo Tahsin slapped a picture of Saddam with his slipper,
demanding, "Why? Why did you do that to us?"
Saddam tried to bargain out of his own death:
he wanted to be shot instead of hung.

Mobile phones have become widespread in Iraq
along with text messages
of flirting
of threats
of kidnappings
of suicide bombings.

Internet cafés fill with Iraqis
asking their relatives for help
to get out of the country.
My old neighbor sends me an e-mail
that her husband has been kidnapped.
The ransom was $50,000,
but she bargained them down to $30,000.
My cousin tells us
that they are voluntarily imprisoned in their homes.
They do not go out even to shop.
Instead, they pay a man
who does the shopping for the entire street.

Lutfiya Al-Dulaimi was offered refugee status in France
after she was threatened by religious extremists.
"This is not Baghdad, our city," she said.
"Our city has been eaten by the wolf."

Siham Jabbar was shot in the arm.
"That is normal," Siham told me over the phone.

Adnan Al-Saigh returned to Iraq to read poetry
at the Writers' Union. He left again
after being threatened by a preacher.

Baghdad is no longer divided into Karkh and Risafa,
but into two zones: a red one and a green one.
American soldiers wander back and forth between
the zones, disappointed they are not greeted with flowers.

Iraqis around the world celebrated in the streets
and raised the flag
when the Iraqi soccer team won the Asia Cup.
They all screamed with joy at the same time
when the winning goal was scored.
They forgot their sectarian differences
for a moment.

Mazin bends his head to the table and cries.
His niece in Baghdad has been kidnapped.
She is twenty years old.
Masked men surrounded her and pulled her away
from her mother's outstretched hands
into a car. They were like a tsunami.
Iraq is a tsunami in slow motion.
I wake at night and wonder if she is alive
and if she is what her life is like.
To be in a cage of strange hands
can only be a nightmare.

It is a great relief to have my daughter
far away from danger
from clouds like corpses
from kidnappers' masks
from long lines at passport offices
from amputated fingers in the sand.

Larsa scatters the old pictures
and mixes them with the new ones.
She mixes pictures of snowballs in Michigan
with pictures of a round city with two rivers
palm trees
poetry
wars
a thousand and one nights.
Inside that city was our home,
inside the home was our garden
not separated from the neighbors even by a wall,
and inside that garden was a *razqi* flower
I will never smell again.

ومن القلب .. منذ ايام
عمّان عنّى ايام امريكا وانا اكتب ولم
يصلني الى الان سوى بطاقة بريدية
يتيمة واحدة لا تنسى بوصول اي شيء اى
اللهمّ .. افتقدك عنّى الرمق الاخير
افتقد كل شيء فيك وحدّثيني انت
دائماً دائماً على بالي وكذلك اصبحت جزءاً
مهماً جداً من داخلي .. فاين انت وكيف انت
ومتى سأراك ؟!
انا بولاي ان اجيئى ولو بسرقة .. محبتي الى الله رب

مهرجان جرش
للثقافة والفنون

Jerash Festival
of culture & arts

الرقم: ٦٥٠/٧/٥
التاريخ: ١٩٩٥/٤/٢٦

الأستاذة الشاعرة دنيا ميخائيل المحترمة،

تحية طيبة وبعد،

يسعدني نيابة عن اللجنة الوطنية العليا لمهرجان جرش للثقافة والفنون ورئيستها جلالة الملكة
نور الحسين المعظمة أن اوجه لكم الدعوة لحضور المهرجان لعام ١٩٩٥ وتقديم قراءات
شعرية من أحدث انتاجكم الشعري.

سيقام مهرجان الشعر هذا العام في الفترة من ٢٢ تموز الى ٢ اب ١٩٩٥. ونحن اذ نتطلع مـع
جمهوركم الواسع الى مشاركتكم نأمل أن يصلنا ردكم قبل بداية شهر أيار القادم.

وتفضلوا بقبول فائق احترامنا،،،

ليلى شرف
نائبة رئيسة اللجنة الوطنية
العليا للمهرجان

الصديقة دنيا ميخائيل
34671 Pisces Dr.
Apt. F, Sterling Hts.
MI 48310, U.S.A
أمريكا

AIR MAIL
PARAVION

با حب

ومنزارون لتقي فيه

المعهد العالي للموسيقى 20 شارع باريس تونس
هاتف وفاكس: 230343

96

بسم الله الرحمن الرحيم

الصديقة العزيزة المبدعة دنيا ميخائيل

طيبه

... البين لاعنا الزمن الأسود الذي رمانا في هذا الـ... بـ
... بعد أن مرت عليه مجزرات الدكتاتورية لتختلف فوقها
أمانـ... في ذهني منصبة نشرتها (الأقلام) من صدق قتل ... ا
... وقع في يد عدد هائلة من المثقفين التي تصدر ن ... طين ...

الأردن - عمان
شركة المشرق العربي للصحافة م.
ص. ب. (٩٦١٨٣٠) عمان ١٩٦

IRAQ POSTAGE العراق ٢٥ فلس دينار

... ريم ... (بابل) بإيجاز ما ادمي صدر من ا، وأنا
... اعتبرول من فئة المرتزقة، الذين يعانون، على ...
... أزمة الخزال
... مرت أ ...
... داخل ... من
... ولتبوا فها نذل اكبيرة
... لصقه من صفات، علينا ...
... إنه هطل على الكو واب

الشاعرة دنيا ميخائيل
لا استطيع ان اصغي الى الخارج

■ حين دعتني الى تناول الشاي في حديقة منزلها .. ادركت منذ اول خطوة في البيت ان دنيا تريد من الاشياء التي حولها ان تحدثني .. حيث تمدد باسترخاء شديد جدار الحديقة ليزاوج حديقتها وحديقة الجيران، سقط الجدار .. اكتفت دنيا بهذا الاعلام غير ان سقوط الجدار لم يكون سوى سقوط شعري - هل رأيتم جدارا نائما .. انا رأيت جدارا يغفو ويصدر شخيرا في حديقة الشاعرة وانا لم ابغ ايقاظ الجدار من نومته العميقة التفت الى دنيا معزيا بمساحة الحرية التي اتاحها سقوط الجدار واجريت معها حوارا استعملت معاولي لتهديم جدران ار واحنا المتكلسة.

والحق اود ان اسجل ان الحوار مع دنياهو حوار مع شاعرة كبيرة بعمر صغير ...

خالد مطلك

■ بعد يوميات موجة خارج البحر، هل سكن البحر او نفقت الموجة.. شاطىء اكثر فولاذية؟

... ماكبيرا مع الطريقة التي تطرح فيها هذا .. بصورة خاصة لا اجد مسوغا للاستعمال ... فولاذية، واذا سمحت لي ان اتلقى السؤال .. لماذا اكتب الآن »بعد يوميات موجة خارج ... غيرك .. ويبدو انني لا اخبيء شيئا..انني .. جديد الذي يقترب من مناخ بيوميات ... أثره بتجربة الحرب وميله الى الافادة من ... بياتية الشخصية ... يغ متفق عليه ... المزاج الذي ... طبيعي لان شم ... قد تقلص الا ... يعني انني ربما

ان بدأت تتعايش معنا او في داخلنا الى الدرجة التي لا نتخيل فيها انفسنا من غيرها .. كما يختلف الكتاب ايضا من ناحية تنوعه اسلوبيا بين الشعري والقصة والحكاية والسيرة والرسالة.

● اعتقد ان ارق النسمات التي تهب من ربيع الحرب هي اكثر فولاذية من ظهيراتنا المسالمة .. لا اريد ان اماحك هنا .. فانني بدور المتلقي الذي تشظت عليه يومياتك فهشمت زجاج امنه وطمأنينته وعادت به الى حيث الكارثة اسأل: هل هدأت عندك الكارثة تماما؟

- استذكر قولا لموريس بلانشو :«لا تتكلم عن الكارثة ،دع الكارثة تتكلم فيك» . وفي الحقيقة ان قول بلانشو هذا هو المفتاح

حبيبتي الغالية دنيا

قبلة حارة بحجم شوقي اليكِ .

جنوات كلّ لوازها دهوراً وأنا افتقدك .. ١
على ابداً ، تختبئين في حبوبي .. أو تتعلقين بأط
أشعر كما لو أنكِ قد ضعتِ بين خطوط يدي
لأستحضرك .. فنأسّس رائعة بريّة .

دنيا ، أحبكِ بكل ما لدي من طاقة على الحب . نما
مل ارتشفكِ أنها الزهرة البريّة العزيزة ..

Dunya Mikhail
4671 Pisces Dr.
..t. F, Sterling Hts.
, 48310, USA

AUSTRALIA 5c Leadbeater's Possum

AUSTRALIA

PAR AVIO
AIR MAIL
INTERNATIONA

48310/3333 53

دنيا ، أيها المسيح في قلبي
أين أنتِ ؟
اكتبي لي ارجوك

DUNYA MIKHAIL

DIARY OF
A WAVE OUTSIDE
THE SEA

يوميات
موجة
خارج
البحر

translated from the Arabic by
Elizabeth Winslow and Dunya Mikhail

A New Directions Book

الجزء الأول
١٩٩١–١٩٩٤

في طفولتي كنتُ أحسد نفسي لأني طفلة.
كنتُ أظن ان كل شخص يُخلق هكذا.
يُخلق طفلاً أو شيخاً أو أُماً.

كنتُ أحزن لأجل أمي لأنها - بحكم سنها- لاتقدر أن تعبث مثلي بالرمل
أو تقفز فوق السرير أو تختبئ تحته
أو ترمي الحصى في البحر لترى الدوائر تكبر حد التلاشي.
فكنتُ كل يوم أُصلي وأحمد الله لأنه خلقني طفلة.

عندما كبرت، لم استطع التخلص من أن أحسد نفسي المعبأة بالطفولة.

كنتُ أعدّ الأحلام بأصابعي وأبكي لأن عدد أصابعي لم يعد كافياً!
كنتُ أبكي أيضاً حين أراني في الصور
وأصرخ: أخرجوني من الصورة!

في فضاء لامتناه من الذكريات، تترامى آلاف الأشرطة الموسيقية
وصور فوتوغرافية هائلة.
كل صورة تأطير للحظة هاربة.

ولأنني لا أحبُ الأطر، كسرتُها كلها لتخرج منها آلافُ الأشياء
والناس
والنجوم
والطيور
واللحظات
متناثرة في أفق رمادي مكسور.

. . .

في طفولتي، رسمتُ جيوشاً من الغبار
ووشاحاً يتهاوى خلفها.
رسمتُ عدداً لايُحصى من المرايا
وأحلامي التي انعكستْ فيها.

رسمتُ البحر
وكائناتي التي ماتتْ فيه.

رسمتُ القمر
وعزلتي التي تكورتْ حوله.

رسمتُ رحيلك
ودموعي التي ارتكبتُها لأجلك.

رسمتُ أجنحة
لأرحل معك

والخ.

. . .

في طفولتي.. جلب لي أبي رقعة شطرنج قائلاً: هذه هي الحياة.. أبيض وأسود.
حين رقد في المستشفى، كان كل شيء أبيض: الجدران، الشراشف، صدرية الممرضة ،
قلب أبي وجليد الأطباء.
وحين خرجتُ من المستشفى، كان كل شيء أسود: الوقت، ملابس النسوة، الصور، الليل
والنهار.

حين طال غياب أبي
بكيت
ماكنت أبكي غيابَهُ
كنتُ أبكي حضوري!

. . .

والحبيب غابَ أيضاً
والشمسُ
والقمر.

ذات مساء .. لا .. ذات صباح .. لا .. أدري .. ذات انتظار .. مرَ الموتُ من أمامنا مثلما كان يفعل كل يوم، ولم أكن وحدي أنتظر بل النهر أيضاً والدخان المتصاعد من الانفجارات ومن سيجارة عاشقٍ يتأمل وحدته مثل بيدق في زاوية الرقعة، فضلاً عن ضجيج الوقت يدق على طبلة أذني مثل عازف مبتدىء، شخير الخوف وأنين الاشجار.
على الرغم من ذلك، غفوتُ لأراك في حلمي.
وعبثاً بذلتُ جهدي لأظل في دائرة الحلم.
وحين صحوتُ، تحسستُ نبضَ قلبي لأتأكد من وجودك!
كان حبك يمشي متعثراً على الضفاف، لكني كنتُ أعرف ان أحلام الحجر هي وحدها التي لا تتصدع وقلب الحجر وحده الذي يبقى.

يدعوني الآخرون لأن أكنسَ عن جثةٍ غبارَ أيامك
وأدعوك لأن تناديني
لا لأجيب أو لأظهر
ولكن لأني أحب نداء احبائي لي.

عندما قلتُ يوماً: أحبك
كانت أحلامي تنهض من قبرها وتتراقص حول الكلمة
وعندما رأيتك يوماً وأنت تبتعد – حتى صرت أبعد الي من نفسي – رأيتُ أحلامي تلك وهي تعود الى قبرها.

. . .

ظلك يجلس القرفصاء على عقارب ساعاتنا ويدور .. يدور .. مثل رأسي .. لا .. ليس مثل رأسي .. بلى .. مثل رأسي .. آه .. أين تقع الأرض؟ من المؤكد انها لا تقع في الذاكرة.

تزحف الشوارع، تتقاطع في عروق يدي.
تختلط في الذهن ملامح المدينة.
تختلطُ الأسماء
الوجوه
الأقنعة
التواريخ

الفصول.

من أين لي القدرة على ترتيب كل هذه الأشياء في الذاكرة؟

قالوا:- لماذا لا تبادرين بالتحية حيت ترين أحداً أمامك؟

في اليوم التالي.. لوحتُ بيدي طويلاً، ولم أجد أحداً أمامي!

. . .

تحوم حولي الذكريات مثل الذباب بطنينه الصاخب.

كلها أسف وأخطاء تشكل منجزات الخراب اليومي الذي علمني ان لاشيء يملك ظلاً بحجم الذكريات الا اللحظة التي يتحول فيها الخشب الى ربابة.

رسمتُ أخطائي فراشات وسلطتُ عليها النور لتحترق.

تراجعتُ.. عرفتُ ان للأخطاء فضيلة تلك الرؤية الموجية التي تلطم شاطيء الحواس السبع فتجعل الاوراق تتناثر وتجتمع وتضج بالهواجس والأسئلة، فنعيد حساب بعض الاشياء الضائعة، ليس بسبب اللامبالاة وانما من فرط ضوئها الدامس مثل وردة تموت من فرط العبير.

وكلما ازداد الظلام تتضح الرؤيا.

الطرقات

الأشجار

الأنهار

النوافذ

كل هذه الأشياء التي لاتعرفني، أعرفها جيداً.

انها تشبه دمعتي لحظة ظل زائف.

تقول الاغنية: "لو كانت الارض مربعة

كنا اختبأنا في احدى الزوايا

لكنها كروية

لذا علينا مواجهة العالم."

هل تعرفون اني كنتُ أطير؟ نبتتْ لي أجنحة، انظروا!

كنتُ سأعلو أكثر لولا الممحاة التي مرتْ على الأفق.

وفي اللحظة الفاصلة التي التقت فيها السماء مع الأرض، خرجت تلك الروح الهائمة من الجسد الأرضي المتعفن لتهيم في مملكة اللاوجود. وقبل أن تصل الى هناك، ارتطمتْ بالغيوم فامتلأ الفضاءُ بغربتها وأحلامها وذكرياتها التي تنهمر ويحسبونها مطراً. في لحظة الارتطام تلك ، تفتت الرأس فانطلقت من انسجته ملايين الطيور فوق بحر من الانكسارات التي تتداعى مثل طائرات ورقية فلتتْ خيوطها فحلقت فوق النجوم الممتدة أمامك ولعل ذلك يفسر ارتباط النجوم بالظلمات.

".. ورأيت النجوم متعلقات كتعليق القناديل في المساجد
ثم صعدتُ الى السماء في أسرع من طرفة عين، فاذا هي سماء من دخان
وفي اليسار رأيتُ شجرة عظيمة ما عليها ورقة الا عليها اسم..."
وكانت الورقة التي عليها اسمي قد تساقطت عن غصنها متخذة شكل طائر.
أوراق خضراء وأخرى صفراء
تساقطتْ عن أغصانها
عليها أسماء تعرفها
وأخرى لا تعرفها.

. . .

كيف سبيل العودة الى الارض؟
الأرض فيها عصافير تنقر في الذاكرة
لذلك الذاكرة مثقوبة.
أريد أن أضع قدمي على الارض
لأعرف قانون الجاذبية.
فهنا .. في الأعالي .. لا جاذبية تسندني ولا ذكرى.

انه انعدام في الوزن وفي التفكير وفي كل شيء..

هل يحق للموتى انتحار ثان ؟
وهل يضمن ذلك عودةً الى الأرض؟

كيف وأنا محض روح ترفرف فوق أشياء لا أعرفها
وأمكنة ليست موجودة؟
كيف تفجرّ كل هذا الغياب في داخلي؟
وكيف أنفقتُ روحي بكل هذا البذخ؟

أريد قليلاً من الأرض تحت قدمي.
مازال كل منا – أنا والأرض – يعتقد انه دفن الآخر في داخله.
ترى من منا فعلَ أولا؟
ومن أجلسَ الشمسَ على عتبة القلب هكذا
ليظل متوهجاً ليل نهار؟

كل يوم أحملُ نفسي
أرشُّ عليها الماء
لعل هدوءَها يأتي.

يُخيل اليّ أحيانا ان الحرب قد انتهت
فتدب الحياة في جباه الجثث لحظة واحدة..
لحظة واحدة تكفي..
لحظة بحجم طلقة..

هل توقفت الحرب فعلاً؟
آه.. هل يتسع العمر لكل هذا اللهاث؟
هل توقفت الحرب؟
ماذا سنفعل الآن بلا أعداء؟!

. . .

تجولتُ بين الانقاض
مثلما تتجول الكلمة في القواميس
لتبحث لها عن معنى
فتراها لغة خالية من الافعال
وتراني فعلاً ماضياً عبثاً تحوله الى مضارع.

قالوا: خلف كل نافذة، مهما كانت صغيرة ، يتراءى أفق ما.
منذ أن سمعتُ ذلك وأنا أرسم نوافذ
لاتفضي الى شيء أبداً .

رأيتُ العصافير تكتب يومياتها.
تقول انها تقتات على قلبي.
تقول ان حبة عشق واحدة
تكفي لتقتات عليها مدى العمر.

أفتحُ نافذة القلب
تطيرُ منها كل العصافير
تذهب الى الحرب لتعشش في خوذ المقاتلين المعبّأة بالذكريات والقمر

في الحرب تجفل الذكريات

أقبض كفي على وطني
أبسطها
لاشيء غير لهاث
وطلقة بلحم الاماني
وحلمُ طحين
يركضُ العمرُ ورائي
أختبىءُ
لكنه حين يفر من أمامي
أتبعهُ
لألملم عن وحشته
هذا الطير المتناثر – وأنا بعضُ رعشته –
أمنية واحدة تكفي
لنترك الأبوابَ مشرعةً للنهار
ونسمّي الشمسَ شمساً
أمنية واحدة تكفي
ليتصاعد الكونُ من القلب مثل البخار
في البدء كانت الأماني

تحملني وتدور بي
أحملها وأدور بها
ندور.. ندور
تدور الليالي
والأماني تبقى أماني.

...

ذات صباح بارد، شعرتُ بأني اليوم سأموت.
فهيأتُ نفسي للموت تماماً
أكملتُ قصيدتي الأخيرة
رتبتُ كفني
واشتريتُ بعض الأزهار لينثروها عليّ
فكلانا – أنا والموت – نحب الأزهار.
قلتُ لنفسي: هل نسيتُ شيئًا قبل أن أموت؟
تذكرتُ أني لم أضع علبة الشطرنج في مكانها
وخفتُ أن يزعلَ منّي الملك
فوضعتُ الأحجار في مكانها على الرقعة.

في فجر اليوم التالي.. رأيتُ الأحجار تتراكض نحو الملجأ وهي تفكر: "لماذا علينا
الاختباء في الملاجيء بينما السماء صافية؟"
تكوّرنا في زاوية واحدة
من دون أن ندري انْ كنا نرتجف برداً أم خوفاً من "الكيمياوي."

في غرفة بيضاء
كان الثلج في داخلنا يلامس قلب الظلمة.
بدت لي الجدران ترتفع من حولنا شيئاً فشيئاً
والسقف ينخفض فوق رؤوسنا.
اجتمعتْ كل الاشياء
وتكورتْ حول نفسها لتتخذ شكل قذيفة
موجهة نحو هذا الرأس الذي تحول الى سلة مهملات.

وقبل أن أعتذر للقذيفة
عن الفراغ الشاسع في رأسي
تطايرتْ أنسجةُ الدماغ مع الذكريات عصافيرَ جريحةً
وأخذتْ تستطيل فوق الرأس مثل شاهدة.

في زاوية ضيقة من القلب
تلمستُ لحظةً هي العمر كله.

كان البرق في الخارج والداخل
رمال متحركة ترتمي بين نبضة وأخرى.

- لكني لم أجد آثارَ أقدامكَ
- هل نسيتِ أني جئتُ محمولاً؟

. . .

حين بدأ العدُ التنازلي،
تحدثتْ قارئة الفنجان عن يوم القيامة
وأنا أفكر : لماذا اذن لم تتحقق الأشياء التي روتْها لي جدتي ذات يوم قائلة أنها مدونة
في الكتب؟
ألاً يتحتم على التاريخ أن يفرغ ما في جعبته
قبل يوم القيامة هذا ؟
ولماذا لم تقل لي جدتي أنّ أيامنا ستوضع في المعلبات
وأنّ الناس سينحشرون في بقع صغيرة مثل سمك المعلبات
وأنّ تكنولوجيا الحلفاء المتطورة ستحاول التهامنا بدل المعلبات
وأنها ستعلنُ ساعة الصفر المئوي فترتعش "الراء" من البرد – الراء التي تفصل ما بين
الحب والحرب.

حدث ذلك في ١٧-١-١٩٩١ فجراً أو ليلاً، فالليل يليق بالكوابيس وبالقمر الذي – بحكم
موقعه القريب من الطائرات – أصبح شاهداً على كل ما يسقط – كان كل شيء يسقط .
وكم بدتْ صورته شاحبة حين انعكستْ في مياه دجلة ذلك المساء!

كانت شجرة العيد ماتزال هناك على الرغم من مرور اسبوعين على قدوم السنة الجديدة
التي كأنها تغشّنا فلا تقدم لنا ٣٦٥ يوماً بالتمام.

كانت الأشياء في الداخل والخارج تضيء وتنطفىء مثل شجرة العيد
وكنا متكورين في أحدى الزوايا
ترتعشُ الراءُ في فجرنا وخرابنا وحرائقنا.
كنا في أيدي الحلفاء مثل علبة سجائر
وكلما مضت الدقائق بدبابيسها ازدادت نسبة الدخان في المدينة..
كنا نتناسب عكسياً مع الدخان وطردياً مع الشموع
كنا نستنشق الموت ونحدق مثل الدمى الى لا مكان.

رأيتُ جارنا البستاني يزرع البنزين في الحديقة
هل سينبتُ الحريق؟

خزانات تُملأُ بالبنزين وبالأسئلة
ومقالات تتحدث عن نظرية موت المؤلف والنخيل.

عينان مسمرتان على شاشة التلفزيون

والبلدُ عصفورُ مخنوق
بين قبضتين تتصافحان بشدة.

المذيع يتلو نشرة الأخبار
وفقاعات تخرج من فمه.
تمرُ الطائرات فوق صخرة "اكو" فيهتزُ الصوت في الأغصان.
النجوم تسقط..
ترددُ "اكو": تسقط.. تسقط..

مُلأَتْ الخزانة ببنزين وخوف وارتباك..
ذهبنا الى قرية تلكيف.
رأيتُ الكلدانيين يسهرون على أغنامهم حتى في الحروب.
في غرفة بلا سقف جلستُ أنظر الى الديكة

وهي تتقاتل فيما بينها من أجل أشياء غير مفهومة.

"ليس للانسان فضل على البهيمة.. كلاهما يذهب الى مكان واحد" هكذا يقول سفر الجامعة.

كانت القرية أصغر من مقبرة

وأوسع من كوكب الزهرة الذي سقط في تنور خالتي

لذلك كان لخبزها طعم الورد.

مرةً أخرى

ننحني

لتمرَ من فوقنا الحرب

هم جالسون بهدوء أمام شاشاتهم الالكترونية

يدوسون زراً

ليشطبوا أجنحتنا الممزقة

قبيل تحليقنا المنخفض فوق خرائبنا.

يدوسون زراً آخر، فتنطلق طائراتهم الينا من جديد

وكأن كل ما غزلته آلاتُهم الجديدة من جحيم

لا يكفي ليعادل جنة لقائنا بأحبائنا من جديد.

تُرى ماذا كان شعور بابا نويل القرن العشرين

وهو يحمل كيس الشظايا الى أطفال العراق؟

وماذا كان شعوره حين أعادوا اليه الكيس محملاً ببعض الهدايا، منها اصبع مبتور وضفيرة حمراء وأشلاء كتاب ودمية مهشمة وبطاقة احتجاج؟

تُرى ماذا كان شعور النقاد الذين ربطوا علم الجمال بنظرية الانشطار

وهم يرون القنابل تنشطر فوق مبنى اتحاد الأدباء وهو يغازل أكاديمية الفنون الجميلة،

فوق جسر الجمهورية وهو يرمي في النهر، مضطراً، كل الوعود التي همس بها الطلاب

لحبيباتهم، فوق شارع الرشيد "أبو النهار" و شارع أبي نؤاس "أبو الليل"،

فوق تمثال السياب بجيبه المثقوب أصلاً،

فوق كلكامش وهو يفتش بين الأنقاض عن الخلود؟

في ذلك المساء حين اقترح المطرُ عليَ دمعة

فكرتُ بشعراء الثمانينيات وهم يغنون أجنحتهم المؤجلة
وبصديقتي هدى التي تقول ان الورود تذبل بسرعة حين لا نهديها لمن نحب.

كانت عقارب الساعة تتفتت
مخلفةً حيواتٍ من ظلمة ورماد وانكسارات حادة في القلب- حين قشرتُ الانكسارات وجدتُ
في داخلها انكسارات.
انفرطتْ حباتُ القلب
وأمتلأ الوقتُ بالغياب.

انهم يرتلون النشيج
أقصد النشيد.

تقول الاذاعات أن طائرات الحلفاء تقذف قنابل عنقودية فوق الملاجئ والجسور ولم اسمع
قبل ذلك بغير عنقود العنب.

أيها العمر – الجسر المعلق بين حربين.
ألا يحلو لوردة الآخرين أن تتفتح الا عند بقايا رمادنا؟

الرسائل لا تصل
الهاتف لا يرن
لاشيء سواي يرن
كم الساعة الآن؟
هل انتهت الحرب؟

هل يعودون؟

هل كان في السماء متسع للطيور
حين داهمت الطائراتُ أحلامنا
وحوّلتْ كلَ شيء الى طحين؟

كان ليلاً متطرفاً
فبعض سكانه لم يذق طعم الرقاد

وبعضهم رقد الى الأبد.

وحين تكاثرت البقع الضوئية في الظلام،
فقدت الاشياء التي في الجو صوابها.
لم تكن تعرف هل هي طيور تحولت الى طائرات
أم طائرات تحولت الى طيور متوهجة؟

كان كلُ شيء يهتز..
المدينة والناس الذين في المدينة
والقلوب التي في داخل الناس
والناس الذين في داخل القلوب.
كانت الطائرات تحلق فوق عاصمة تضخ سكانها الى القرى
نحو مصير مجهول
واسئلة أطفال لا يملك لها الكبارُ أجوبةً مقنعة.

طائرات تحلق فوق ساحة التحرير
وترسم الحيرة في عيني جواد سليم
بعد أن هجرتْ خيولُه العاصمة.

طائرات تحلق فوق الملاجئ
فوق الأنقاض التي نبتت في الملاجئ
فوق الأطفال الذين ناموا تحت الأنقاض
فوق الأشلاء التي كانت أطفالاً قبل قليل
فوق الفحم الذي آلت اليه الأشلاء
فوق الجدران التي امتزجت بالفحم
فوق كل قطرة دم على الجدران.

في الحرب، لا أحد ينجو من الموت
فالقتيل يموت جسدياً
والقاتل يموت انسانياً.

في هذا العصر الذي تطفو فيه كلمات مثل: صواريخ.. طائرات.. قصف.. حصار..

عقوبات.. شعارات..
في مثل هذا العصر، لا يكون انتحار روميو وجوليت حباً بل غيظ واستهجان.

دخان
دخان يتصاعد من البيوت المحترقة
ومن سيجارة جندي امريكي يحس بالذنب
ومن ذيل قطة.

من عاصفة الصحراء تهوي طيورُ الفضيحة
والملوك يتسمون لتماثيلهم
ويصلّون: النفط أكبر..
بينما الأنهار تواصل جريانها الطبيعي وكأننا لامرئيون – غائبون دائماً تحت الأنقاض.

الكارثة تسهر علينا في الليل – ليلنا المتكرر الى ما لا نهاية – مما يدلّنا على فعل بلا فاعل ولا مفعول.
وها اننا، عبثاً، نحاول أن نقفز فوقها – فوق الكارثة.
فنسقط من لا مكان في كل زمان.

نتعرف على الموت في غير وقته
ولا أحد يستخدم "الفيتو."

أنت تفكر، اذن أنت تعرف الكارثة.

قرأتُ مرة أن المفكّر الفرنسي موريس بلانشو قال:
في حين تنتزع منا الكارثة هذا الملجأ الذي هو فكر الموت وتصرفنا عن المذهل أو الفاجع وتغنينا عن كل ارادة وعن كل حركة، لا تتيح لنا، اضافة الى ذلك، أن نجازف بهذا السؤال: ماذا فعلتَ لكي تعرف الكارثة؟

. . .

في ١٦-١-١٩٩٣ ليلاً ، عادت الطائرات
بنعيقها المربك وصفارات انذارها..

في البداية ظننتُ أن ما اسمعهُ هو من تأثير الاستذكار
وأنّ الأصوات التي ترن في اذني منذ سنين قد تعالت حتى خرجت من الورقة الى الهواء.

رنّ الهاتف. كان صوتُ شاعر على الطرف الآخر:

- ألو.. هل سمعتِ الأخبار؟
- أي أخبار؟
- لقد سقطتْ طائرة.. وهل ذهبتِ الى المطبعة؟ وهل...؟

تعالتْ أصواتُ الطائرات
وخفتَ صوتُ الشاعر.

أغلقتُ السماعة وأنا أشعر بأنّ السماء لا بد ان تسقط يوماً فوق رؤوسنا.
عادت طائراتهم تدس مناقيرها في هوائنا.
أحدثتْ في جدار القلب ثقباً
من هذا الثقب يمكنك أن تشاهد الكارثة.
هم جلبوا القير والسمنت
وأغلقوا الثقب
أغلقوه بإحكام
لكنهم أبداً لن يتمكنوا من اخفاء الخراب الذي وراءه.

في يوم ما، سيأتي بعض الفضوليين
ليفتحوا الثقب من جديد
ويتفرجوا على بقايا الانهيار.

بلى، أيها الطيار، يمكنك أن تحطم الانسان في الظلمة
ولكن هل بوسعك أن تهزم الليل
الذي سيهبط الى قلبه ؟
بلى، يمكنك أن تقتل الانسان بآلاتك المتطورة
ولكن هذا لا يعني انك هزمته.
ألم يخبرك همنغواي بذلك؟
بالمناسبة، رأيتُ همنغواي البارحة وقال لي: من وجهة نظر الطبيعة، ليس هناك فرق بين

موت انسان وموت ورقة شجر.

لم يصدقني حين حكيتُ له عن عودة الطائرات الى سماءٍ لما تزل تلتمع من الحزن وتنثر دموعاً سوداً الى الارض التي وقفتْ أمام المرآة عابسةً بعد أن أشار اليها طفل وقال:

لست أجمل الكواكب.

بدتْ منتفخة لكثرة ما ابتلعتْ من الشهداء.

القمرُ هجرها

فحزنتْ كثيراً وصارت تدخن بإفراط.

اختنق بنو البشر وظلوا يسعلون.

دخان.. دخان يتصاعد من بقايا الأشياء..

تسللَ الدخان الى القبور

فمتى تبتكرون موتى لا ينفذ اليهم الدخان؟

الأرض خانقة وبعيدة عن بسمة الطفل.

لا خفة الريش ولا الأحلام تكفي

لحملها بأقفاصها الزجاجية

كل زجاج مشروع انكسار.

كان القفص المتدلي من عمود في باحة دارنا يشبه المشنقة.

في القفص اربعة عصافير لا تزقزق – لم أدرِ إن كانت حزينة أو خرساء.

واحد منها مات بعد أيام قلائل – هكذا من دون أن يتفوه بشيء.

دفنتُه في الحديقة.

وبعد أن غرستُ في ترابِ زهرة حمراء بمثابة شاهدة،

سمعتُ، لدهشتي، زقزقة متواصلة تنبعث من براعم الأزهار

ومما زادني دهشة انني حينما تقدمتُ لأقطف أحد تلك البراعم،

رأيتُ قطرات من دم على أوراقها.

فركتُها لأتأكد مما أرى

فامتلأتْ يداي بالريش.

في الليل، فتحتُ باب القفص

ترددت العصافير الثلاثة في مغادرة مكانها

ساعدتُها بأن أمسكتُها وبسطتُ يدي

الى الفضاء الواسع أمامها.

أخرجتها واحداً تلو الآخر
وكأنني أنقذُ مملكة من الهلاك.
حدقتُ اليها وهي تطير
ومن فرط نشوتي تركتُ باب القفص مفتوحاً.
في صباح اليوم التالي، سمعتُ جدتي تقول ان القطة قد اكلتْ عصافيرنا الوديعة.
تذمّرتُ: لا تسلمُ العصافير حتى وهي في القفص.

وكنتُ كلما وجدتُ طائراً في قفص
أتحولُ الى جدران أربعة.

. . .

في احد ايام الأعياد ، أذكرُ أني ذهبتُ الى الكنيسة
وخرجتُ من بين جموع المصلين الى شمعة في العراء.
وقفتُ أتأملها حتى ذابت متخذة شكل طفل في حضن مقلوب.
تقدم نحوي شخص يرتدي البياض
أعطاني الكتاب المقدس قائلاً انه رأى في عينيّ بريقاً غريباً.
قلتُ ربما لهب الشمعة فعل فعلَهُ.
لكنه أوحى الَي بأنني قد أصبحُ رسولةً ذات يوم.
بقيتُ مشدوهة مدة غير قصيرة
لا أتكلم ولا أفعل أي شيء.
كنتُ أفكر كلما رأيتُ شخصاً أعرفه:
تُرى ماذا سيكون ردُ فعله اذا تحقق كلامُ الرجل ذي البياض؟
منذ ذلك الوقت وأنا أنتظر من دون جدوى ملاكاً أو وحياً
يبلغني برسالته حين أنام.

كانت احلامي أو كوابيسي تتكرر:
نجوم ترتجف في البحر
وأفق يبتعد مثل صدى..

مرة رأيت حجارةً هائلةً تتدحرج من مكان مرتفع
وأجنحةً تتناثر

مثل جيش مهزوم.

كمثل السائر في نومه
نمضي الى الحرب
ونغط في قمامة عميقة.

. . .

كان الطفل يهيء قبضته في الحلم
وهو يسمع نداءً متكرراً:
اضربْ أعداءك..
اضربْ.

نهض الطفل يسأل أمه: ما الأعداء ياأمي؟
- أنهم أولئك الأشباح الذين يقفون خلف الخط موجهين بنادقهم الى القمر.

- لكن القمر مشترك بيننا وبينهم
فهل يضربون الجزء الذي يخصنا؟

- أجل.. أحياناً يصيبون الهدف
فيسقط نصف القمر أو أكثر
فيصير هلالاً
وأحياناً يختفي.

- هذا يعني انهم أحياناً يصيبون النصف الذي يخصهم ايضاً ياأمي

- نعم، وهذا مايُسمى بالتضحية.
يضحون بما لديهم
من أجل القضاء على مالدينا.

- وماذا يربحون ياأمي؟

- يفسدون علينا الفوز

- ما الفوز؟

- يكتبون علينا الخسارة

- ما الخسارة؟

- خسارة الفوز أو فوز الخسارة

- متى نغادر؟

- الى أين؟

- الى حيث لايسقط القمر.

. . .

البارحة سقط القمر في التنور
ونضج مع الخبز
فأخطأتُ في صلاتي هكذا: أبانا الذي في السموات
اعطنا القمر كفافنا اليوم...
أردتُ تصحيح العبارة فاكملتُ: واغفر لي اني أكلتُ القمر.

أعرف انك في كل مكان لكني أرقب أغنيتك وكأني انتظرُ مفقوداً.

كل يوم، نكتبُ أمنياتنا في وريقات صغيرة ونضعها في كيس.
هل صحيح ان الشيطان يأتي كل يوم ويأخذ الكيس الى الجحيم؟
اوقْفْهُ ياأبانا.. اوقفْهُ في الطريق.
ولكن لاتنثر علينا الاوراق،
انها ثقيلة.
وحتى إن لم تكن ثقيلة،

يكفي انها تجعلنا نحس بأننا نكذب،
نكذب على أنفسنا .
أنت أوصيتنا أن لانكذب يا أبانا.

جنودنا نبتوا في الأراضي البور
وبعضهم طار الى السماء ضارباً الغيوم- التي ظنها الأعداءَ- بأجنحته المدببة
مسبباً سقوط المطر من عيون الأمهات.

ماذا قلتَ لهم بعد أن فتحتَ السماءَ؟

بلدنا ينام وهو واقف
زمنهُ يمشي واقفاً
قلبهُ يدق واقفاً
فلنقف دقيقة حداداً.

آه.. يا بلداً يملك ابرة (حادة، رقيقة، واخزة)
من خرمك
يدخل التاريخ
وتخرجُ خوذ مثقوبة

اهتزازاتُ متكررة تجري على أرضك
وكأنّ أيادي خفيةً تهزُّ أشجارَك ليل نهار.

حاصروك وطردوا ذرة الاوكسجين عن مائك
وابقوا ذرتي الهيدروجين تتعاركان.

أما كان ينبغي للشعوب أن تضطرب أمام طفل يغلق فمه وعينيه
باستسلام أمام قرارات الأمم المتحدة؟

لكنها اكتفت بأن فتحت فمها قليلا- أقل مما تفعل البراعم-
وكأنها تتثاءب أو تبتسم.

وجعلْنا لكل نجمة مكاناً في نهارنا
وأبقيْنا موتانا بلا قبور

كتبْنا جميع أسماء الورود على الجدران
ورسمْنا الحشائش- طعامنا المفضل- نحن الخراف
ووقفنا نفتحُ أذرعنا للهواء حتى نبدو مثل الاشجار.
كل ذلك من أجل أن نحوّل الأسوار الى حدائق.
ثمة نحلة ساذجة صدقتْ فأرتطمتْ باتجاه ماظلنتهُ زهرة
أما كان ينبغي للنحل أن يطير أعلى من الأسوار؟

طوابير طويلة أمامنا.
واقفين.. نعدّدُ الطحين بأصابعنا
ونقسمُ الشمس في الأواني المستطرقة.

ننامُ واقفين في الطوابير
ويفكرُ الخبراء في تصميم قبور عمودية
لأننا سنموت واقفين.

نحن ديكور ينقصه كل شيء.
موجودون لولا وجود السياسة.

أزهارنا تتسلق الجدران في الحلم.

أرامل يحلمن بلقالق تقذف بالغائبين من المدخنة.

ويتامى يدخلون الأنفاق معتقدين انها قبلات طويلة.

كل يوم نحمدُ الله، ونتلقى بصقةً من الشيطان
اذ نصلي من أجل الوطن- فردوسنا المفقود.
كل يوم يملأون الجرار بحروفٍ أو حروب
كل يوم نكسر الجرار.

تجارُ الحروب يبيعون الهواء
ويمجّدون أوسمةً من تنك
وبناتٌ يمشطن الحنطة كل يوم
وينخلن الغيوم في الأواني
فيبزغُ القطن على رؤوسهن فجأة
مثلما تبزغ الثوراتُ بثوب أبيض
فلا تعرفُ البناتُ إن كان كفناً أم ثوب عرس!

. . .

لم يصدق الشهيد عينيه عندما قُصف قبرُه
وهو يضفر اكليلاً لحبيبته
أحمر أكليلُها
لكنه، في الطريق الى السماء، تحوّلَ الى بياض.
ينحني الى الماء ممسكاً بقوس قزح صغير
هكذا يعزف.
يرفع يديه الى الغيوم ويضفر من دمعها زهرة
هكذا يغني.

موجة تتكسر خارج البحر
هكذا أمضي.

. . .

أحلم أن أذهب الى مدن بعيدة،
كانت معلمة الجغرافية قد أشارت اليها في الأطلس.

- ما الجسر؟ تسألني
- الجسرُ انحناءةُ أمام طفلها المتساقط مع أوراق الشتاء الميتة،
دمعتها ارتعاشة طيور مبلَّة.

- ما الشط؟

- الشط قلب لم يحتله أحد
ومع هذا بقي ممزقاً بين جميع من ادّعوا سيادتهم عليه.

سلالاتُ جاءت وانقرضت والشط يلعب بالحصى،
غير مبالٍ بكل الحروب التي تجري على ضفتيه.
مرات يقول لنفسه: يالهم من حمقى، هؤلاء الرابضين دوماً على يميني وعلى يساري.
هل أرمي بهم الى الحصى التي كانت في قديم الزمان أجدادهم؟
هذه الحصاة الكبيرة ذات النتوءات كانت يوما ملكاً
وتلك البيضوية الملساء كانت أميرة
فمتى يعرف اولئك الحمقى انهم في النهاية
سيستقرون كلهم عند أقدامي؟

. . .

تجمعتْ شظايا الزجاج والحكايات والطيور وصيحات الناس
حول تلك المرأة في فندق الرشيد.
كانت ميتة.

كم موحش كل صخر لا تطلع منه زهرتك
يابلدي
وكم تذبل!

. . .

أراد الأب أن يفعل شيئاً من أجل أطفاله
فأرسلهم جميعاً الى الملجأ
ونام
رآهم في الحلم ملائكةً شفافة تخرج من فوهة بركان
تيبّسَ الدم في عروقه قلقاً حتى تحوّلَ الى حجر صغير
جاء طفل ورمى الحجر بالمقلاع فأستقر عند فوهة بئر
وبذلك أصبح مُطلاً دوماً على هاوية سحيقة.

. . .

أطفال الحي يطرقون أبواب الليل طلباً لشمعة

والبيادق ينسحبون من الرقعة بلا أحذية ولا أحلام.

هذا عالم يؤمن بالديمقراطية لذلك مُنِح الموتى حرية التنزه في المدينة.

دائماً أقوم من مكاني وكأنني بصدد أن أفتح النافذة.
ربما ولدتُ لأفتح النافذة
أو لأتنزه.

وحدي أحصي الحروب- الأشجار
التي نثرتْ ثمارَها أمام الأطفال
أكلوا منها فشاخوا مباشرةً.
مُرَّةٌ ثماركُم
فمتى تربون الأطفال بعيداً عن الأشجار؟

. . .

الموتُ دائماً يشتاق الينا
انه يأتي من وراء القارات
يقطع المسافات الطويلة وسلة النار في يده
يعطينا كرات من النار لنلعب بها
فننسى معنى الشمس!

ظلّ الطفلُ يبحثُ عن قمر شاحب
رآهُ ذات يوم قرب النافذة.
ربما سقط في النوم (ما النوم؟)
ربما أكلتهُ الديدان (ما الديدان؟)
ربما اختفى مع الكهرباء (ما الكهرباء؟)
ربما هدأت العاصفة

ربما لم تهدأ بعد.

قالوا: املأوا الصناديق بالهواء (شهيق وزفير ولا شيء)
لمن ولماذا نخزن الهواء؟
لا ثمار تحمل تاجنا
ولا ظلال تعكس وجودنا.

ضجيج يملأ المكان وكأن علبةً قد فُتحت على حين غرة
فخرجتْ منها أكداسٌ من البشر والسيارات والصناديق
متجهةً الى ما لا نعلم
ولا هم يعلمون.

أيُّ سحر حوّلَ المدينة التي تضج بالحياة وبالحركة
الى أميرة نائمة
تنتظر قبلة الأمير حتى تتثاءب من جديد!

أيّ أيدٍ كانت ترش الموت على الأشجار
فتسقط حبات قمح من مناقير مرتعشة
وتجمد عيون الطير المليئة ببيوض مكسورة
ولانها عيون خالية من السماء،
لم ترَ النجوم اللامعة فوق جسر يتدهور.

لقد حوّلتْنا الالهةُ الى اصنام
لكنها نسيت أن تقتل فينا الشعور
فظلتْ آلامُنا شاخصةً الى الأبد.

لاَ آثار لنا
نحن...
نحن الآثار.

الى أين تسرع بفأسك؟

الحروبُ تتناسلُ
وتقذف بنا الى الخارج
أما الآخر فهو يسير على رؤوس أصابعه فوق قبورنا
عابراً الى حرب أخرى.

. . .

أعرفُ ان يديك خاويتان
أعرفُ ان يديك لا شغل لهما الأن
ولكن هذا لا يكفي لأن تمرنهما على التصفيق

. . .

أنت لا تشبه الليل فلمَ تطلبك الظلمات؟

أين كنتَ حين أسستُ البحر
ورسمتُ السماء بجانبه (لاأريد الطائرات).

أين كنتَ حين أسستُ ظلك
ونقشتُ فوقه دمعتي
فتدفق نهرُ من الشمع في المدينة؟
ظلّ الشمعة يرتجف!

أين كنتَ حين أسستُ زهرة
وطلبتُ أن تقطفها لي؟

أين كنتَ حين أسستُ الكون؟

في البدء كانت خلية أميبة واحدة لا شكل لها.
نفختُ فيها دهشتي فنمتْ أشياء عظيمة ومتناقضة،
حلقّ الهواء حولها،
منحته خفةً لا مثيل لها،

طاب لي ذلك فتلألأتْ نجومٌ من فرحتي
أمسكتُها وعلقتُها في الفضاء.
ومن أجل أن أتخلص من فوضى الكتلة الواحدة المضطربة، فصلتُ بينها،
فتدحرجتْ كرتان مشعتان سميتُهما الشمس والقمر،
منحتُ النهار واحدة والليل أخرى.
التفتُ الى جميع أعمالي والى ماعانيتُ من التعب (فاذا الكل باطل وكَبَة الروح)
تأفّفتُ فكانت الريح.
بكيتُ فكان المطر.
نفختُ في المياه أحلامي فسبحتْ أسماك بحراشفها الملونة
وفاضت البحارُ عن حيوات متنوعة.
منحتُ الطيور للهواء والدواب للأرض
ثم أخذتُ حفنة من التراب وعجنتها بدمعي،
نفختُ فيها فكان كائنٌ يشبهني.
أكملتُ لوحتي واسترحتُ في اليوم السابع الذي قدسته بأن جعلته عطلة
أصابني الملل فمزجتُ النار والهواء والماء و التراب
وها أني أشمّ رائحة الأنقاض.
ندمتُ على جميع أعمالي فرسمت الطوفان
ولبثتُ سبعة أيام أُخر قبل أن "أطلقَ الحمامة من التابوت."

ارتفعت المياه حتى كادت تغرق السفينة الوحيدة في اللوحة.
سرتُ تاركةً خلفي مدينةً يتصاعد منها البخار.
لكني التفتُ الى الوراء رغم الصوت القائل:
"كلُّ من يلتفت الى الوراء يصير تمثالاً من الملح."

ركضتُ وأقدامي تراوح في مكانها
وفي فمي طعم غريب وأحساس غامض بالذوبان في الماء.

أهـ.. كيف جلستْ وحدها
المدينةُ الكثيرةُ النفط والكروب؟

دمعتُها خرجت تحمل لافتة تقول:
"الحكمةُ خيرٌ من آلات الحرب وخاطىءٌ واحد يتلف خيراً جزيلاً.. "

قلتُ: فلأشطب اذن سلالة النار ولأضرب المياه بعصاي لئلا تنقلب دماً.

ومضتْ سبعةُ أيام
بعدها ضربتُ الماء، فماتت ذرةُ الاوكسجين وتقافزت ذراتُ الهيدروجين تولولُ.
نثرتُ الغبار لعناتٍ على الشعب، فمضوا ثقيلي الأحمال.
كلُ واحدٍ يحملُ وزره.
ومضيتُ أحمل الشعبَ- وزري- وزادت الأحمال حتى غطى الغمامُ البيوت.

- متى نخرج؟
- عندما يرتفع الغمامُ عن المسكن
- واذا لم يرتفع
- ننتظرُ أن يرتفع.

ونفخوا في الأبواق ليرتفع الغمام.
لقد ارتفع، فما بالهم ما انفكوا ينفخون في الأبواق!

خرجوا تتقدمهم توابيت تبحث عن مكان استراحة.
تذمروا وصرخوا: "لماذا أتينا الى هذه الدنيا حتى نسقط تحت السيف
ويصير أطفالنا غنيمة؟"
وارتفعوا الى الغمام.
ارتفعوا...

. . .

منذ متى وأنا هنا
أمتطي "آلة الزمن"؟
أقفز بها الى المستقبل
فأجد نفسي وقد تحولتُ الى جنين في بطن الحوت
سأولد عما قليل
وأكتشف العالم من جديد
آمل أن أعيش هذه المرة بلا كلمات
فهذه الكائنات المدمرة لم تدع لي وقتاً للفعل

وأنما سحبتني الى الأعماق مع باقي السلالات المائية
ويبدو انني سآتي مع مواليد برج الحوت في كل مرة
فها هو اله البحار نبتون
يكتب اشياءه على جبيني.

أعدتُ آلتي الى الوراء بقوة
فرأيت اوتونبشتم يكشف لكلكامش سراً من أسرار الآلهة
قال: "سأَكشف لك ياكلكامش الكلمة السرية
أحكي لك أنا سر النبتة
هذه النبتة كالشوك في أعماق البحار
انْ توصلتْ يداك للحصول عليها
فستحظى بشباب دائم..."

ورأيتُ سيدة الماء
وهي تهبني كلمة السر
من خلال محارة وضعتْها على أذني
ودعتْني اسمعُ شفرة البحر.
قالت: "أردتُ أن آتي اليك بالبحر
ولكنه كان مشغولاً بالأعاصير وعناق الغرقى
وذاهلاً في سكره
لقد ارتشف القمر قطرة قطرة
سرقتُ صوته المخبوء في نبض محارة
وجئتُ به الى الموجة الهاربة
وعلى شرفات الماء، اختطف الحوت عشبة البهجة من يدي
واختفى في اعماق البحر.
هذه حبة رمل نسيَها الحوت على جبيني
عندما قبّلني تحت اقتران المشتري بالشمس ووهبَني كلمة السر الوحيدة."
ظلتْ المحارة تهمس في أذني كل يوم بسر جديد.
قالتْ لي ذات مساء ان النقطة أصل العالم.
حين تثاءبت النقطةُ واستيقظتْ من غفوتها
بعد انتهاء مفعول السحر الذي جمّدَ روحها مُدداً طويلة،
أبصرت الفضاء اللامتناهي حولها.

تحركتْ فتركتْ أثراً هو نقطة أخرى نقيضة.

التفتتْ الى الوراء وقد امتدتْ علاقةٌ - هي خط مستقيم- بين النقطتين.

في منتصف المستقيم تماماً، تجلس قوةٌ مركزيةٌ تحيطها هالةٌ من نور وترفعها ثمانية أسرار بجلال ومهابة.

. . .

نقاطٌ ذكية كشفتْ نصف الأسرار وظلَّ نصفها الآخر عصياً على التفسير.

النقطة المركزية تحتمي بأسرارها المتبقية وتعزم على أن تسدل الستار الكامل لحظة الكشف عنها.

كشف السر هو لحظة النهاية التي تضع الحد الفاصل بين العتمة والضياء، فلا يتناوب الليل مع النهار بل يقتسم الليل نصف الكرة الأرضية الذي أدار وجهه عن الشمس الى الأبد وسيكون النصف الآخر من نصيب النهار دائماً. وسيُطلق على سكان القسم الأول أصحاب النار أو العتمة وعلى سكان القسم الثاني أصحاب النور أو الجنة. أما اولئك الذين يقفون على الخط الفاصل تماماً بين النار والنور فهم في المطهر حتى يُتاح لهم- بفعل نفخة بسيطة- الانزياح قليلاً الى أحد الجانبين.

اذن هناك قوة سحرية جمّدتْ روحَ النقطة

وقوة أخرى مقابلة أعادت اليها الروح فتثاءبتْ.

التثاؤب أول اليقظة وأول الحياة... تعقبهُ الحركة.

الحركة تترك أثراً.

العودة الى نقطة الحركة الاولى تؤدي الى الفناء لأن الازاحة في هذه الحالة تساوي صفراً لذلك فأن لحظة الفناء ستأتي عندما تلتقي النقطة نقيضَها (أو اثرَها) تاركةً موجاتٍ كهرومغناطيسية، وهذا ما يؤكده عالم الكيمياء بول ديريك الذي يقول أن الالكترون ونقيضه يولدان معاً في اللحظة نفسها وفي المكان نفسه ويموتان معاً لو تقابلا في أي زمان ومكان.

فكرتُ بذلك عندما ألقتْ قوات الحلفاء ٨٨ ألف طن من القنابل على بلاد النهرين فظهرتْ في الجو اشعاعاتٌ ملونة مختلفة أنطلقتْ بسرعة الضوء أو الخوف وتركتْ طاقةً لاتُفنى.

هي فكرة قابلتْ نقيضَها فتحولتْ الى اشعاعات تُهلكُ الناسَ والحجارة.

ولكن المادة بفنائها قد حررتْ طاقةً هائلة أربكتْ تجاربَهم وهم يحوّلون صورَنا في المختبر الى النيجاتيف.

يُقال أنّ الميت طاقته صفر لانه لا يستطيع أن يُخرج لسانه أو يحرّك شفتيه.

نحن موتى ونملك طاقة، هذا هو الفرق.

أما هذه الثقوب التي أحدثَتها القذائفُ في الروح وفي الحجر فهي ليست تجاويف فارغة ميتة.

انها تماماً مثل الثقب الذي يتركه الالكترون السالب حيث سيظهر في مكانه، في اللحظة نفسها، جسيم بصورة معكوسة هو البوزيترون الموجب.

هذه الفجوة التي يتركها الالكترون أو القذيفة لها وجود لا يمكن محوه أبداً من محيط المكان.

بل ان اصطدامها أحياناً بجدار الذاكرة يولّد شرارةً حارقةً تومض عكس عقرب الساعة.

تقاطعت الخطوط المستقيمة مما أدى الى انشطار كل نقطة تقريباً الى أعداد كبيرة من النقاط المماثلة التي أخذت تلتقي وتفترق وتهز رؤوسها الصغيرة في الفراغ .

أما النقطة المركزية فقد دخلت في "غرفة الغيوم" التي تتوجه منها المسارات الكونية وصارت تبكي من هول ما حدث فهطل مطرٌ عظيم وتجمعت القطرات ليتكون عالم مائي كبير انبثقتْ منه كتل يابسة هنا وهناك تعلوها أقواس قزح.

تناثرت النقاط، بعضها في الماء وبعضها في اليابسة، وأخذتْ تقوم بأفعال مختلفة أو متشابهة موجّهة من الأشعة القادمة من "غرفة الغيوم."

تمضي النقاط ضمن مساراتها المحددة حتى تصطدم بنهاياتها الصلبة فتتوقف عن الحركة،

أما طاقتها المتبقية –رمادها- فلا تفنى بل تتجسّد وتمر بغربال الضياء فيتحدد دورُها القادم بحسب كمية النور التي تنبعث منها.

أعبثُ بالآلة فتتلاحق الصور وتتراكم الأعداد.

الأعدادُ غريبة- نحسبُ بها ولا نقدر أن نحسبها- ما معنى لا متناهية؟

الأشكال الهندسية لها أبعاد محددة لكنها في الحلم تصبح دائريةً حيث تخرج الروح من بيتها- الجسد- وتتجول في عالم بلا أبعاد ولا نهايات.

تذهب الى الخلف أو الى الأمام فترى أحداثاً قبل وقوعها بدقائق أو أيام أو قرون، فتعيش ومضة المستقبل الذي يكشفُ غطاءه لذبذباتها المرهفة.

أديرُ مؤشر الآلة الى العام ١٩٩١ فتتعرض عتلاتها الى اهتزازات شديدة وتكاد تلتهمها النيران. ياإلهي.. انها تهبط تحت الأنقاض.. انها تتفكك وتنزع عنها تحولات الأحداث والصور مثلما يفعل القمرُ في يدي.

القمرُ دائري (ويصير قوساً أحياناً) وكذلك حبات الأسبرين وقطرات المطر والعجلات والفقاعات (قبل أن تنفجر) لكن الصفر هو وحده الذي يحقق اللانهاية.

لاحظْ أن قسمة أي رقم طبيعي (ماعدا الصفر) على نفسه يساوي واحداً

أي اذا فرضنا (س) عدداً طبيعياً (ماعدا الصفر)

فان س / س = ١

بينما صفر / صفر = مالانهاية.

تمنيتُ أن أدير مؤشر الآلة الى عام صفر ولكن الكارثة التي حللنا عندها قد عطلتْ كلَ شيء

مما جعلني أعجز عن تحريك الآلة الى الماضي أو المستقبل.. بل انها لم تعد تعمل على الأطلاق.

لقد توقفتْ عند هذه النقطة الحرجة من التاريخ حيث درجة الازاحة تساوي صفراً.

. . .

بعربة يجرها خيط دخان

وصلتُ الى لحية جدي التي كان يمسك بها كلما سمع صافرة القطار.

قال لي: "لاتبتعدي كثيراً لئلا تبتلعك نبتةُ غريبة."

تركتُ لحيته الى دولاب هواء علّمَني أن العالم مستدير مثل خوفي.

سمعتْ أمي صافرة القطار وقالت أن أباها قد ابتعد كثيراً

فقفزتُ من حضنها وذهبتُ أفتش عن النبتة الغريبة التي ابتلعت جدي.

قابلتُ الهاوية وجهاً لوجه

وقد أقنعتْني بأني أسير بالمقلوب

ولا أعرفُ الأشياء الاَ بعد وقوعها.

كان القارب مقلوباً وكأنه تكشيرة النهر

لكنّي حين مضيتُ بعيداً صرتُ إحدى أسنان القارب

وبدا الماءُ مبتسماً.

رأيتُ البلاد جميعها في الخريطة

مسكتُها بيدي.

كان طائر ما قد فعلَ "فعلته" على الخريطة

قبل ان ألطخها بالحبر الأبيض.

كم غيمةٍ تنقصني لأمطر أمنياتي على المدن؟

كم هجرةٍ تنقصني لأصنع الآيات؟

لماذا أُلامُ اذا ابتعدتُ عن مرايا تعكسُ ما لاأرغب؟
تُرى، ماذا يحدث اذا فكرت المرايا أن تنظر الى نفسها؟
هل ترمي بنفسها في النهر مثلاً؟

هكذا تمضي حيواتنا...
مثل هذه الانحناءات المائية التي تظهر أيضاً في تخطيط القلب حيث تبرز- عند كل صعود
للخط- عبارة "كيف الحال"؟

لا أُدير خدي الآخر عندما أتلقى صفعةً
لأني أسرح وأرى القمر يسقط مثل دمعة.
القوس متوتر بما يكفي لاطلاق الأغاني .
من جوفي أطلقتُ الأرض بعيداً... بعيداً جداً.

شيءٌ ما يتدحرج في الأفق ويشدُ اليه المعادن جميعاً.
لمعانٌ متعبٌ يدفنُ أرقاماً بلا نهاية.
مكائن تدور أسرع من نبض أحلامنا المخفوق.
أسلحة بأجنحتها السود في طبقة سفلى من جهنم.
أقنعة تتدلى في البرزخ.
أفواه تنفتح وتنغلق مثل مزلاج في باب خشبي قديم
ولحىً تلعب الدومينو مع أهل الكهف بانتظار معجزة.

أمضيت وقتاً من الرحلة في قراءة لوح من سفر "تثنية الاشتراع":
"ويسوقُ الربُ عليك أمةً من بعيد، من أقاصي الأرض، كالنسر المحلق، أمة لاتفهم لغتها،
أمة صلبة الوجوه لاتهاب وجه شيخ ولاتشفق على طفل، فتأكل ثمر أرضك حتى تفنى ولا
يبقى لك قمح ولا نبيذ ولا زيت ولا نتاج بقر وغنم. تبيدك وتحاصرك في مدنك كلها حتى
تسقط أسوارك الشامخة، تحاصرك في كل أرضك التي يعطيك الربُ اياها..."

كنتُ أحرك المجذاف حين مرّ حاملو تابوت على النهر
"فوقف الماءُ المنحدر من الأعالي وقام كتلة واحدة"
رأيتهم يرفعون حجراً قائلين انه تذكار من المياه التي انفلقتْ أمام التابوت.
وما أن نقلوا أقدامهم الى اليابسة حتى رجعت المياهُ الى مكانها
وجرتْ كما كانت تجري.

رأيتهم يحفرون قرب نخلةٍ بها مرض انحناء الرقبة.
أنزلوا التابوت الى الظلمات
ثم سدّوا الحفرة بالحجر (تذكار المياه وهي تنشقُّ).
تناثرَ بعض الرطب على القبر وكأنه يريد أن يحلّي مرارة الموت.

تقدّم رجلٌ من الحجر وأزاحهُ قليلاً
وأخذ يخاطبُ المرأة الميتة التي كانت تتعرض في اللحظة نفسها للحساب
وكانت منشغلة بصياغة أجوبة للسماء.

قال الرجل الأرضي: أنتِ يا من خرجتِ من ضلعي
أما كان حرياً بك أن تعودي
الى هذا الضلع بدلاً من العودة الى التراب؟

قال الصوت السماوي: أنتِ أيتها المرأة
لماذا قبضتِ روحك قبل الموعد المكتوب؟
وماذا تركتِ لملاك الموت أن يفعل؟

قال الرجل الأرضي: أ كان ينبغي ذلك حقاً؟
لو كنت صبرتِ لحظاتٍ فقط
لملأتُ ساعاتِك بقوس قزحي
وبنورٍ ملونٍ كلما لمسته تدفقتْ عيونُ ماء
وجناتٍ تجري من تحتها الأنهار.

قال الصوت السماوي: مَن دلّكِ على المكان الذي لن يصيبك فيه
مرضٌ ولا شيخوخة ولا ملل ولا فناء؟
مَن؟

قال الأرضي: كانتْ لنا أعيادُنا ونجومُنا التي نضيؤها للشجرة
فلماذا أطفأتِ الأنوار وأسدلتِ الستارة على الحياة؟

قال السماوي: لماذا حرّضتِ البحار على الطوفان؟
وجعلتِ زهرة عباد الشمس تلتفت الى القمر؟

والجبل ينتفض من أجل نملة بطيئة لم تصل الى قمته؟

قال الأرضي: اني أتذكّرُ تلك الأيام الحلوة التي قضيتُها في الجنة
قبل أن أعرفك وأُطرد بسببك
ليتني لم أسمعْ كلامك، فما الذي جنيته ُ غير الشقاء؟

قال السماوي: لماذا أغويت رجلك بالخروج من أرضه الطيبة؟
بسببك كانت النار التي عكّرتْ صفو السماء.

قال الأرضي: هل أنا أحد مخلوقات برومثيوس حتى تغضب عليّ الآلهة
وتهدي اليّ هذه "المرأة" التي دقتْ أجنحتي على الحائط
ونزلتْ هي، بكل ثقلي، الى الحفرة؟

قال السماوي: لقد خُلِقَ الطيرُ قبل البشر
لذلك لابد للانسان أن يتخلف عن الطائر
فلماذا خالفت الطبيعة واستبدلتِ بالأجنحة
كل ما تيسّرَ للانسان من عطايا؟

حملَ السماويُ المرأةَ بأجنحتها البيض الى الأعالي
أما الأرضيُ فدخل في الشجرة لينبتَ له ضلعُ جديد.

حدقتُ الى الأعالي
كان نورس يرافق القارب طوال الوقت
ذكّرَني بالنورس "جونوثان" الذي غادر السرب
ليعيش وحده في المرتفعات المطلة على البحر
واكتشفَ ان العجز و الخوف الذي يجعل حياة النورس محدودة،
بسبب القهر الذي يمارسه المجتمع معه،
يمنعهُ من الطيران
لكن النورس "جونوثان" يكبرُ من دون أن يشيخ
بل تزداد طاقاته على التحليق بشكل مذهل
حتى يصل الى السماء...
"فالحمد لله حين يطير، ولهُ الحمد حين يهوي."

أحسستُ بأنني أشفى من جميع أمراضي
وأنا أنظر الى النورس يبسط جناحيه في الهواء
وكل أثقالي تتهاوى وأنا أحلق معه.
رأيتُ ملوكاً يقتسمون الأرض بالقرعة
فعاد ذهني الى الوراء ورأيتني، وأنا في العاشرة من عمري، أقتسم الأشياء بالقرعة مع
أخي الأصغر.
كنتُ أقذفُ القطعة المعدنية، بعد رهانه على أحد الوجهين، في الهواء
لتعود معلنة فوز أحدنا بأشياء لاقيمة لها.
مرةً رميتُ القطعة المعدنية بعيداً جداً
حتى انها اختفتْ ولم تعد الى قطعة الأرض الصغيرة المحددة بيننا
فأحسستُ براحة لا مثيل لها- راحة التخلص من رنين القيد.
طارت القطعةُ المعدنية في الهواء
واستعدتُ أنا حريتي.

بصوت أعلى من نداءات بائعي الماء على الأرصفة
أتلفظُ باسمك أيتها ال ح ري ة (ماء بارد)
بالنيات وحدها تُزاح التلال من أمام المنظار
وتمضي الأشرعة
كان على الشراع وحده جفاف وعلى سائر الأرض ندى.

تحكمتُ بعدسة المنظار
فاقتربت الطيورُ
صارت عدسةُ منظاري هي السماء
(اعتقد الملاك جبريل ان الطيور هوت الى سمائي؟)
وابتعدت الأشجار
صارتْ خطوطاً ثم نقطاً
وانطلقتْ رصاصاتُ الصيادين الى الهواء بحرية تامة
(لم يقف شيء في طريقها)
صار منظاري هو البندقية الوحيدة الموجهة الى الطيور
لكنها بندقيةٌ تطلق رؤى بلورية شفافة كاتمة للصوت.

رسامٌ واقعي في الخلف هزّ رأسه حيرة وهو يقلد الطبيعة.

في اللوحة كان طائر هائل على شجرة متناهية في الصغر.

أخذ يفكر برسام آخر مجدّد كان قد قال له بان الطبيعة هي التي تقلد الفن.

أشفقتُ على الرسام الواقعي الذي فقد صوابه أمام الأبعاد الجديدة

فغيرتُ عدسة المنظار وقربتُ الأشجار حتى بدتْ بحجمها الطبيعي

وأصبحتْ مهدَّدة مرة اخرى بثرثرة الطيور

والطيور مهددة ببنادق الصيادين

كانت الأشجارُ- قبل تدخلِّ الواقع- قد عاشتْ حيواتٍ مثيرة تُخرجها من صمتها أمام الأجيال.

فعندما صارتْ نقطاً، دخلتْ في "سفر القضاة"

وجلستْ على الحروف مثل عرش أخضر.

قالتْ لشجرة الزيتون: كوني علينا ملكة.

فقالت لهنّ الزيتونة: أ أدعُ زيتي الذي لأجله تكرمُني الآلهةُ والبشر

وأذهب لأترنح فوق الشجر؟

فقالت الأشجارُ للتينة : تعالي أنتِ وكوني علينا ملكة

فقالت لهن التينة: أ أدعُ حلاوتي وثمرتي الطيبة

وأذهب لأترنح فوق الشجر؟

فقالت الأشجار للكرمة: تعالي أنت وكوني علينا ملكة

فقالت لهنّ الكرمة: أ أدعُ نبيذي الذي يُفرح الآلهة والبشر

وأذهب لأترنح فوق الشجر؟

خرجتُ من "سفر القضاة" وأنا أفكر: أ أدعُ حريتي وأذهب لأترنح فوق البشر؟

. . .

ترنَّحَ القارب وكاد أن ينقلب

لأنَّ الاله "زيوس" أخرجَ عاصفةً شديدةً من صندوقه السحري.

لقد جمعَ حوله حاشيته ليشاورهم في طرائق إبادة البشر.

وقد طرب لاقتراحاتهم ومنها طوفان

وبروق

ورعود

وحروب.

أشار الى ورقة الحرب وأمر بتنفيذها.

احتشد الخلقُ في بقعة مرتجفين بينما كان هو يراهم من عليائه محض نقاط سود.

كان أفراد حاشيته يضربون على الآله الكاتبة

بالسرعة نفسها التي تقصف بها طائراتهم الأرض

كانت الأرض تترنح تحت القصف مثل سكّير.

في الصباح، شرب "زيوس" البحرَ وأكل حورياته نخب الانتصار

وفي المساء تغوّط قمامةً عظيمةً من القاذورات التي تجمع حولها الذبابُ.

ضربَ بعصاه السحرية على طيور البجع

فتحولتْ الى خفافيش متوحشة تنبىء بالقادم قبل وصوله

وتُصدرُ أصواتاً مخيفةً كلما حاول كائن أن يفلت من المدار.

انها تطلق كل يوم آلاف الأصوات التي تؤدي الى اختفاء آلاف الكائنات.

أحدهم سمع حشرجات في الأسفل

وعندما وضع اذنه عليها

عرفَ أن الأرض عبارة عن صَدَفة.

في احدى ردهات الصندوق، هناك نسيج عنكبوت هائل

وعليه تلتصق أجسادٌ وأحشاءٌ بشرية.

جاء "زيوس" ووضع اطاراً حول النسيج

فصارتْ لوحةً فريدةً للفرجة.

وفي ردهة أخرى، يوجد حوض أسماك كبير.

الأسماك معلقة من زعانفها بخيوط تتدلى من سقف الحوض

فهو يتضايق من حركتها السائبة في الماء.

في أوقات الفراغ، ينشغل "زيوس" بقص النجوم من السماء

ولصقها على الأكتاف.

ويبدو انه كثيراً ما يمارس هذه الهواية

بدليل ان السماء قد فقدتْ أخيراً كل نجومها.

كانت نموره تروح وتجيء في أقفاصها

في الليل تلتهم الغنائم

وفي الصباح، عندما يمرّ هو من أمامها، تموءُ.

هذه النمور تُلقي دروساً في فن الترويض

أمام جدار عليه صورة الاله "زيوس"

وهو يحمل سوطاً في يده وذهباً في اليد الأخرى.

مسلته‍ُ السوداء باضتْ عليها الأفعى ما لا يُحصى من القوانين

فكلّ كلمة يتفوهُ بها بيضةُ أفعى.

هو يملك مرآة سحرية

ينظر اليها فتنعكس صورته في كل الجهات

لذلك فهو يُرى في كل مكان في وقت واحد.

انه يسمع كل شيء في كل لحظة

واذا نزلت لعناتُه وتعالى زئيرُه فانّ كارثةً تحلّ في المكان.

وأذا أشار للنور قائلاً هذا ظلام فأن النور لن يرى النور أبداً .

لقد ألبسَ بعضَ كائناته خرقاً ذهبية

ونصبهم في الحقل بمثابة فزاعات

وكم تحس هذه الفزاعات بالوحشة فلا أحد يقترب منها أبداً.

كلما بعث بأحدى صواعقه من الصندوق،

قدّمَ الحشد نذورَه من الذهب والفضة والبنين

ومجّدَ تاريخَ الصاعقة بابتهالات عامة كل سنة.

هياكل عظمية تعثرتْ في مسيرتها اليه

فأخذ يعزف عليها بأنامله

ويستخرج الأناشيدَ من جوفها الفارغ .

قبل يوم القيامة ،أرسلَ زيوس أحدَ أفراد أسرته وهو برومثيوس لسرقة النار من جهنم

فأتاهُ بها مرتجفاً.

حكم زيوس على سارق النار بالموت حرقاً
ثم قدم هديته الى البشر حمماً بركانية تتوهج هنا وهناك.
خرجت الجموعُ وفي ثيابها النار تحيي الحرائق ومشعلي الحرائق.
في جولاته الى الأعلى، تنحني الآلهة
ويصعد أحدهم على أكتاف الآخر
ليتمكن هو أخيراً من الصعود الى ابليس.

مرةً وضعَ الجحيمَ في جيبهِ
ونزلَ ينثر على البشر شراراته الجهنمية.
مدَّ يدَه للتحية فنزل عليها المطر.
أحد المجانين صرخ بان الغيمة تبول في يده.
أمر زيوس بإحراق الغيمة على مرأى من الجميع
ونثرها في البحر.
وحينما اضطربت الموجاتُ حزناً، أحاطها بأسلاك شائكة.

. . .

على شاطىء البحر كانت صَدَفة كبيرة
بداخلها بروتوبلازما الشعر.
أحد ما أتى بها اليّ وربط مادتي الحية بخيطها اللامرئي
فشعرتُ بأني طائرة ورقية
تنظر الى العالم من فوق.
وأني، كأي طفلة، أشياء صغيرة تجعلني أحلّق أو أهوي.

صَدَفة الشعر هذه سحبتْني من أو الى كل شيء
ولم تدعني أفعل شيئاً غير العبث معها وتمجيدها.

وقد حاولتُ مراراً التخلص من قوتها المغناطيسية ووطأتها الشديدة عليّ:

أولاً، مارستُ رياضة اليوغا
لإفراغ ذهني من كل مايتعلق بها
لكنها استغلتْ حتى هذا الفراغ أو اللاشيء وحوّلته الى شيء خاص بها.

ثانياً، جلستُ مع نسوة عديدات
لعل أصواتهن تتداخل مع تلك الثرثرة المائية
التي تطنّ في أذني طوال الوقت
ولكني لم أسمع شيئاً من أحاديثهن
لأن ذهني كان غزالاً شارداً.

ثالثاً، أعلنتُ توبتي
وتلوتُ "فعل الندامة" أمام الكاهن الذي قال: "اعترفي بالمزيد."
اعترفتُ: "لقد دخلتُ في التجربة."
رسم أشارةً معينة فوق رأسي
وجعلني أصلّي
لم يكن يدري ان الصلاة بطقسها الانفرادي
لا تختلف عن فعل الصَدَفة الذي جئتُ أتوبُ منه.

رابعاً، فكّرتُ أن أدحرجها على الرمل
لكن نواتها الثقيلة وفعلي المتكرر ازاءها
جعلني اعتقد بأني أحرك صخرة سيزيف.

خامساً، لجأتُ الى عرّاف
لعلّه يخبرني متى سينقطع الخيط.
تمتمَ بكلماتٍ مبهَمة
ونظر الى كفي قائلاً
انه يرى خيطاً عميقاً واحداً تحيط به خطوط واهية
مثل خربشات.

سادساً، مسكتُ بها لأرميها في البحر
غير اني وقفتُ مبهورةً بسحرها وجمالها
وقد أخذني بهاؤها كأني أراها للمرة الأولى.

سابعاً، دخلتُ في مثلث برمودا
لعله يمتص ذبذباتها الصوتية،
لكنه اتخذ شكل صَدَفة كبيرة احتوتني بداخلها.

وبعد أن باءت محاولاتي بالفشل، جاء ذلك "المجهول"
وأغلق علينا الباب، أنا والصدفة،
وقد أوحى صوت المفتاح الى أن الهرب محض خيال.

بيد أن الصَدَفة حملتْني، وكأنها مركبة فضائية،
الى كوكب آخر مليء باللآلىء والأعشاب البحرية
كوكب مائي ليس فيه شيء ثابت قطّ
بل خلايا أميبية قابلة لاتخاذ مختلف الأشكال والأحجام .

هل يمكنك أن ترسم أمطاراً لاتهطل
وريحاً لاتتحرك؟
ذلك مارأيته هناك.

ورأيتُ أيضا أحجاراً كريمةً
تعلوها اشراقات فذة وشموسٌ ورقية.
كانت هناك أنهار في كل مكان
ولم يكن العبور عليها يحتاج الى جسور أو الى اية وسيلة أخرى.

أما سكّان الكوكب
فيحملون جراراً مثقوبة يملأونها من مياه النهر
وعلى الرغم من احساسهم بعبث ما يقومون به،
لا يملكون الاَ أن يحملوا جرارهم المثقوبة
والذهاب بها الى النهر كل يوم.

استلقيتُ على الماء في اغفاءة قصيرة
رأيتُ في اثنائها نفسي وهي تطوف في كوكب الأرض
وتتحدث مع الناس عن كواكب أخرى.
أخبرتهم بأني الآن في الحلم واني لا أستطيع أن أراهم الاَ من خلال هذا الحلم.
قلتُ لأحدهم اني أعيشُ في صدفة كبيرة
واني آتي هنا كلما أغفو.
قال اني صحوتُ توّاً
لكني بقيتُ أحدّثه عن حياتي التي هناك

واني الآن هنا حسب طول الحلم.
جلب ابرةً وحقنني بها.
لم أعترضْ لان الألم ليس حقيقياً في الحلم
ولم أبالِ لأن كل شيء سيزول حالما ينتهي الحلم.

هناك في الجانب الآخر، تفجّرتْ من الصدفة براكين ماء
غطتْ أعماقاً من ظلمة ونور
ثم هدأتْ وانحدرتْ الى احدى السواقي.
بين خطوة وأخرى توجد ينابيع
لذلك يكفي أن تسير حتى يتحول المكان الى نافورة.

الطبقات الجوية في الصدفة خاصة بالأطفال
لذلك لا يمكن لمن يكبر أن يعيش فيها.
أطفال لا يفهمون القوانين
ولا يجيدون غير اللعب
واطلاق بالونات وأسئلة.
يمضون ولا ينتظرون جواباً أبداً.
يدحرجون الأناشيد الزئبقية الى أمام
ثم يملّون منها
فيهجرونها في آوان مستطرقة مهمَلة
فتفقد الأواني خصائصها وهي تحوي الأناشيد غير المستقرة أبداً.

يضربون قوس قزح بسهامهم
فتنبعث موسيقى ملونة
تساوي الصمت في قيمتها وبهائها.
لهم عيون عجيبة
تستطيع رؤية أصغر الأشياء والذرات
من دون عناء أو مجهر.
بنظراتهم تتدحرج الصخور
وكل ما يلمسونه يصير زهرة
طوفان من الأزهار حملوه من الصدفة الى الجنة.
ينزلون الى النهر فتتجدد أوراقهم التي تعكس، على صفحات النهر،

كلّ ما تطيّرهُ أيديهم في الآفاق
يلوّحون بمناديلهم الشفافة
فتخرج منها كلمات فوق بنفسجية
تبرز أيديهم فوق الماء
وكأنهم يوشكون على الغرق
ولكن ما أن يهرع مخلص اليهم حتى يدرك انها أيدٍ لاتجيد التعلق بأية قشة
وانها هكذا مرفوعة دائماً وكأنها تحيّي الأبدية.

يمشون على الماء
خالي البال والأيدي
يكتشفون العالم وكأنهم جاءوا توّاً الى الدنيا
وفي اليوم التالي يكتشفونه من جديد
يملكون عصا من الآس
لا يشيرون بها الى شيء محدد
إما لأنهم لايعرفون الحدود
أو لأنه لاتوجد نقطة ثابتة يمكن الاشارة اليها.

أطياف من عصور سالفة نقشوا رسوماً على الجدران.
مررتُ من أمامها فنهضتْ من غفوتها الطويلة
وحيتني بإيماءات رقيقة
وابتسمتُ لها.
قلتُ سأنقش رسومي أنا على الماء
لأضمن لها توتراً ابدياً.

ليست هناك عبارات معينة يتم تداولها في عالم الصدفة المائي
فبإمكانك أن تقول مثلاً ان الساعات عاطلة عندما تريد ان تقول ان الظلام سيحلّ بلا
نجوم هذي الليلة
وأن تقول أن الأسوار لا مبرر لها عندما تريد أن تغازل الوردة
وأن تقول ان الغيوم ملأت المكان عندما تريد أن تقول إنك نسيت.

النسيان هو مهنتي هناك
ومن المصاعب التي تعترضني انني كلما أغفو وأنزل في حلمي الى الأرض،

يسألني السكان عن التفصيلات
وهم لا يعلمون انني كنتُ، طوال الوقت قبل ان أراهم، لا أفعلُ شيئاً غير النسيان.
لذلك تراني أكرر لهم دائماً ان الغيوم ملأت المكان.

عندما تموت اللغةُ، يدفنها الأرضيون في القواميس
بينما لا تملك اللغة قبراً في عالم الصَدَفة.

احدى اللواتي زحفنَ من كوكب الماء الى كوكب الأرض
(بفعل عوامل بيئية بحتة)
قرأتْ في القاموس انّ "الشعر" كلام موزون مقفى.
لم يكن الشعر يخضع الى تعريف في اثناء حياتها المائية السابقة
ففي الصَدَفة، كانت ربّاتُ الشعر يضعنَ الشحنات الشعرية في سلك غير مرئي
وما أن تستدلَّ عليه حتى يغمرك الضياء أو تموت.
وأدرك البرمائي ان الشعر اذن قد تحول، على يد واضعي القواميس الى الحالة الغازية الى
الحالة السائلة ثم الى الحالة الصلبة
بينما التسامي هو التحول من الحالة الصلبة الى الحالة الغازية من دون المرور بالحالة
السائلة اصلاً.

رميتُ القاموس في البحر
وتأملتُ الكلمات وهي تكبر مع الدوائر وقد كساها الملح.
كانت الحروف تغيّرُ أمكنتها
فيتحول الـ م ل ح الى ح ل م
كانت الحروف تُمسك بعضها بعضاً
وترقص في حلقات دائرية بلا نهاية
مثلما تظهر الكلمات على شاشة حديثة لا تتدخل فيها الأصابع.

ولم أفعل أنا شيئاً.

في يوم من أيام طفولتي، وأنا أرمي الحجر في البحر،
ارتبكت الحروف والدوائر
وفلتتْ من أيدي بعضها بعضاً
انتشرتْ حروف الـ ب ح ر، وهي في قمة اضطرابها،

وتجمعتْ أمامي على شكل ح ر ب

قوةٌ رهيبة دفعتني من أو الى بطن الحوت
فعرفتُ انَ الجحيم هو ألا أصحو من الحلم أبداً.

لقطاتُ كثيرة مرتْ من أمامي.
لقطاتُ غير مترابطة وكأنها مقتطعة من ملايين الأفلام.
لقطةُ أناس يبتسمون في وجهي
ولقطةُ آخرين ينظرون اليَّ شزراً.

واحد يمسك بيدي ويسحبني وراءه مبتهجاً
وآخر يرفع يده ثم يُحدث صوتاً وألماً في وجهي.

أيدٍ تلوّح
أو تتوعد
أو تقيس الحرارة.

تمرُ لقطةُ نسوة يلطمن
ويرقصن حول صندوق خشبي.

أحدهم وضعني في صندوق زجاجي
فرأيتُ أشكالاً هندسية متكررة
تتخللها لافتات سود وأضواء باهرة.
بعضها أضواء محايدة وأخرى منحازة
تأمرني بالسير أو الوقوف.
لم يتبدل اللون الأحمر
وحين حاولت أجتيازه، تبعثْني صافرات وتكشيرات متقنة.

لقطات كثيرة مرتْ من أمامي.

لقطة بيدق في المربع قبل الاخير من الرقعة
في انتظار النقلة التي سترشحهُ الى أي شيء آخر.

لقطةُ رجل ثلج بخوذة وهو يطفر فوق النار.

لقطةُ غصن يرتجف في عين طائر.

لقطة طائرة تلتهم القنابل ثم ترميها من مؤخرتها الى الأرض.

لقطة قمر ينفجرُ.

أمضيتُ وقتاً طويلآ هنا، بيدي شمعة
لا تنطفىء أَبداً
ولا تذوب
مما يدلّ على انني ما أزال في الحلم.

مثل قصيدة هايكو

حقيبتي اختزلت العالمَ الى صورٍ

ورسائلَ ودفترٍ وقلم.

لاوقت لترتيب الطاولة وقد تراكمت فوقها قصاصات ورق عليها ملاحظات وأرقام هواتف فوق طبقة من الجرائد والمجلات، مع فتاحة الرسائل التي لاأملك لها صبراً فأنا أفتح الرسائل بسرعة البرق.

تركتُ كاسباروف على الجدار وهو يلعب الشطرنج، فهو، على أية حال، لم يعرف انه كان فارس أحلامي وقت المراهقة.

تركتُ كتبي كلها ماعدا "الأمير الصغير."

انما أخذتُ الرسائل والصور

ولو احتلت الحيّز الأكبر من الحقيبة.

ثلاثون عاماً من عمري

مررتُها بصعوبة

من فوق عتبة الباب الى الخارج.

لاأَدري كم مرة عبرتُ تلك العتبة

لأخرج أو أعود

من المدرسة أو الجامعة أو الشغل أو السوق

أو اتحاد الأدباء أو مطعم أرض سومر

أو نادي السينما أو بيت الجيران.

انتابني شعور مزعج وأنا أغادر

بأَني لابدّ نسيتُ شيئاً ورائي.

لكنني قررتُ ألاّ أنظرَ الى الوراء.

مضيتُ وبداخلي مشاعر اورفيوس وهو يخرج من العالم السفلي.

لن ألتفتَ الى مدينة مثل هذه: جميلة، قبيحة، محبوبة، مكروهة، قوية، ضعيفة، ساخنة، باردة، قاسية، حنون، حميمية، ولامبالية.

غادرتُ بذاك الشرط الواحد: ألا أنظر الى الوراء.

ما كان بامكاني الهروب الا بشكل قانوني.

ذلك يعني لابد من وجود "مَحرَم" أي رجل من العائلة يرافقني الى خارج البلد

وكذلك الحصول على اجازة غياب من المكان الذي أعمل فيه (جريدة بغداد اوبزرفر).
أستخدمتُ دعوتي الى مهرجان جرش للثقافة والفنون في الأردن لأنفذ من قانون المحرم،
واستخدمَ خالد م. "وساطته" في دائرة الجوازات.
غيّروا مهنتي في الجواز من "صحفية" الى "شاعرة."
الشعر لايستدعي اجازة من أي مكان.

خروجي من البلد حدث مثل أي شيء آخر في العراق: صعب ان أرادوه صعباً وسهل إن
أرادوهُ سهلاً .

كانت القوانين الشفاهية أهم من القوانين المكتوبة مابين النهرين.
قانون لايسري على الجميع، في نهاية الأمر.
أردتُ أن أغادر قانونَ دولة الى دولة قانون.
أردتُ أن أحمل بغداد (بغدادي) الى اميركا
وأدمج الاثنين معاً مثل طين اصطناعي لأصنع "بغداديكا"، بغداديكا الحرية والوفرة
والجنون،
بغداديكا الشرق والغرب.
بغداديكا عشتار تحمل كتاباً بيد وشعلةً باليد الأخرى.

حذرّني صوتٌ قادمٌ من البرية بألا أضيع في أرض جديدة من أجل حلم
بألا أضيع في لامكان مع لاأحد باتجاه لاشيء.
بعضهم وصلوا معبئين بالأحلام، ولكن من شدة التعب أدركهم النوم فاستفاقوا دونما
أحلام.

كنتُ معبأة بأحلام هي المح في بيضة مسلوقة
وكنت أخشى أن تلتهم الحروب ماتبقى من صفارٍ
فخرجتُ من البلد وأنا أفكر بأن الحياة ربما هي في مكان آخر.
رددتُ: في مكان آخر، أي مكان آخر، ولأكن مثل الذكريات: لاتبالي أين تسكن وكيف
ومتى ولماذا.
لأقع في البئر وأُنسى.
لتلتمع في عيني ملايين الأحلام العامة البراقة، لايهم، سأغلق عيني لأرى أحلامي الخاصة
الصغيرة.
لتشرق عليّ الشمس وتغرب كل يوم بحيادية تامة.

ذلك هو شغلها، في نهاية الأمر.

. . .

– " ماكل هذه الأوراق؟"، يسألني مفتش الحدود في طريبيل.
أتلعثم ويدي على قلبي خشية أن ينتزع شيئاً من الحقيبة
فأقول له: "سأحضر مهرجاناً شعرياً. تعرف ان الشعراء يتحدثون كثيراً في المهرجانات.
أجل.. يتحدثون كثيراً ويحتاجون الى الكثير من الأوراق."
هناك، بين بغداد وعمّان، تسحبُ نفساً عميقاً دائماً حين يتركك شرطي عراقي تمضي
لشأنك.

امتلأت الساحة الهاشمية في مركز عمّان بحقائب ووسائد أنزلها عراقيون من الباصات غير
واثقين فيما اذا كانت هذه محطتهم الأولى أم الأخيرة.
طغت اللهجة العراقية على شوارع المدينة ومقاهيها مما دعا عراقياً طريفاً يعلّقُ حين رأى
أردنياً في الساحة الهاشمية: "ياه.. ماذا يفعل هنا هذا الأردني؟"

دونما رخصة عمل، اشتغلتُ في جريدة أردنية مستقلة تدعى "المشرق."
كان لي فيها عمود أسبوعي بعنوان "خربشات."
ذلك ماأفعله عادة: أخربشُ.
رئيس التحرير، م مشاركة، يبتسم لي عادة كلما سلّمتُ عمودي الساخر.
هو يحلم أن ينام مئة سنة ثم يصحو فيجد بعض ديمقراطية في الوطن العربي.
في غرفة الأرشيف، هيّأوا صوراً تتماشى مع المواضيع:
اجتماع لرجال عقلاء يصنعون خططاً
حكّام يلقون خطباً عن التقدم والأزدهار
احتفال بالذكرى الخمسين لتأسيس الأمم المتحدة
عطايا الحليب للاله شيفا
دواء جديد للصداع
ألبوم جديد لكاظم الساهر
معرض رسومات ومنحوتات القارة الأفريقية
هياكل ديناصورات
لاجئون يهربون من أوطانهم
ضفدعة تنتقل الى مستنقع آخر

حرب باردة تنتهي وحرب ساخنة تبتدي

دمية مهشمة بين الأنقاض

خريطة مجعّدة

رجال يتصافحون

بعد العمل في الجريدة، أذهب عادةً الى مقهى الفينيق حيث ألتقي بأدباء عراقيين خرجوا بدورهم من البلد. كان عبد الوهاب البياتي يجلس هناك دائماً في المكان نفسه يحيط به شعراء شباب. لم يكن يبدو لي بأن أحداً منهم كان ينوي العودة الى العراق.

"على الأقل لا أحد هنا يطالبني بهوية وأنا أسير في الشارع،" قال لي م النصار.

وسام (ة) بدا وكأنه يريد أن يقول لي شيئاً. أخذني جانباً وقال لي: "أنا سعيد لأنك خرجت من البلد. أريد أن أبوح لك بسر. في أحدى صفحات ملفك الأمني في العراق، كانت هناك علامة استفهام حول ولائك. كان هناك تساؤل حول ارتباطك بجماعات مسيحية خارج العراق. كنتُ مكلّفاً بالملف تحت التحقيق. لكن، كما ترين، هربتُ أنا أيضاً."

اذن كان موالياً لهم؟ لكن ليس موالياً بما يكفي. استدعيتُ مناخ قصائده التي كانت حداثوية وذات مواضيع عامة. لا أتذكر أي واحدة تعبوية أو مدّاحة للسلطة.

احتسيت قهوتي التركية و قلبت الفنجان على الصحن الصغير للمرأة التي تقرأ الطالع و تفسّر الأشكال التي تركها البن في فنجاني. أردتُها أن تخبرني بأني سأقابل شخصاً يساعدني، أي شخص.

بعد اسبوع تقريباً، قال لي رئيس التحرير بأننا مدعوون مع صحفيين آخرين الى حفل عشاء في السفارة الأمريكية بمناسبة رأس السنة. سألني فيما قدّمتُ الى السفارة الأمريكية للحصول على تأشيرة بعد.

- "لم أقدّم بعد. سمعتُ بأنَ الطابور طويل وأن التأشيرات للعراقيين متوقفة في كل السفارات."

- "حسناً. أعتقد انَ حفل الاستقبال فرصتك. من يدري؟ سأعرّفك الى شخص قد يساعدك."

- "شكراً. ذلك فضل كبير."

- "أنت تستحقين الأفضل."

في خضم الاحتفال، عرّفني رئيس التحرير الى مستر فان، موظف امريكي هندي الاصل.

"اسمك معناه العالم في اللغة الهندية،" قال لي.

"له المعنى نفسه في اللغة العربية،" أخبرتُهُ.

قال: "تعرفين صعوبة اعطاء تأشيرات دخول للعراقيين هذه الأيام."
لم يستطع أن يعدني بشيء انما طلب مني أن أجلب جواز السفر.
بدا لي مستر فان مثل أبطال الأفلام الهندية التي كنتُ أشاهدها مراراً مع أبي في سينمات بغداد أيام الطفولة. كنتُ دائماً أحرج أبي بالكثير من الأسئلة فلم أكن أملك صبراً لمعرفة ماذا سيحدث. ولكن، عند النهاية، كان البطل دائماً يعود الى حبيبته، فأتنفسُ الصعداء لأنه لم يكن ميتاً مثلما تصورتُ.

. . .

ذات صباح عندما أصرّت بعض العصافير على ايقاظي مبكراً اذ ظلت تنقر بمناقيرها على زجاج نافذتي بالحاح غريب وكأنها تود أن تنقل لي خبراً، كانت تأشيرة الدخول جاهزة لي.
لم أعرف كيف أُغيّر ملابسي في ذلك الصباح اذ كنتُ قد نمتُ الليلة الفائتة وأنا أرتدي تقريباً كل ماامتلكتُ من ملابس. كانت غرفتي مبنية فوق سطح بناية مائل بسقف يوحي بانزلاق ما. والمدفأة الصغيرة هناك لم تكن لديها مهمة التدفئة، انما تسريب غاز يساعد على السعال فحسب. كنتُ متجمدة و لم أملك غير الشمس لتدفئتي.
مستر فان ختمَ جوازي بالختم المطلوب، ولم أستطع أن أشكرهُ فلم يكن هناك عندما تسلمتُ الجواز.

كانت صحيحة تلك اللعبة، لعبة الوردة، التي كنتُ سليتُ بها نفسي. تقطف ورقة لنعم وورقة ل(لا) فتتوقع أن تحصل على ماتريد مثلاً اذا كانت الورقة الأخيرة نعم وهكذا. تحتاج عادة الى رقم فردي. تعلمتُ تلك اللعبة من بنت الجيران في المرحلة الثانوية. كانت تقطف وردة وتقطع أوراقها واحدة واحدة وهي تكرر: يحبني، لايحبني، يحبني، لايحبني. كانت تحب صبياً في المنطقة. ماكان أهلها، على أية حال، سيسمحون لها بأن تتزوجه فقد كان مسلماً وهي مسيحية.

أخذتُ جوازي فوراً الى دائرة البريد لتسلّم الرسالة المسجّلة التي كانت بانتظاري لأكثر من شهر فقد أصرّوا على أن أريهم جواز سفري أولاً. شعرتُ بغضب على دائرة البريد لأنهم رفضوا أن يخبروني باسم المرسل، وشعرتُ بغضب على السفارة الأمريكية لأنهم احتفظوا بجواز سفري لديهم لفترة غير محدَدة. ولكن كل ذلك حلّ محله الآن شعور بالامتنان اذ استلمتُ رسالتي وبيدي الجواز والتأشيرة.

كانت الرسالة من بغداد مرسلة من صديقتي لطفية الدليمي. ضمت شفرة خطيرة محتواها: "الأزهار ذابلة." كنا اتفقنا على استخدام كلمة "الأزهار" كوسيلة للتخاطب في زمن الرقابة، ففهمتُ بأنها تحذّرني من العودة الى العراق.

رسالة أخرى جاءتني من صديقة سويدية اسمها ايفا. كان كلامي مضطرباً وموجزاً عندما أجرتْ معي حواراً صحفياً في بغداد. موظف من وزارة الثقافة والاعلام كان جالساً أمامنا في استعلامات الوزارة. كان يرافقها "لتسهيل" أمورها. طلبتْ مني أن أصاحبها في اليوم التالي الى اثار بابل. أتذكّر نظرتها المنتشية حينما التقطتْ حجراً صغيراً من أحجار بابل وقرّرتْ الاحتفاظ به كذكرى. قال لها المرافق ان ذلك حجر عادي لاقيمة له، فابتسمتْ وقالتْ: "لاأصدّق بأني أمشي على أرض بابل التي طالما قرأتُ عنها في كتب الأساطير." كنّا نسير بين تماثيل الأسود والثيران المجنّحة حينما أشارت ايفا الى تماثيل "السيد الرئيس" قائلة: "ياترى، هل سيحطّم الناس في المستقبل هذه التماثيل مثلما حدث مع ستالين؟" حمدتُ الله لأن المرافق لم يسمعها تلك اللحظة ثم همستُ في أذنها بأنّ الأفضل ألا تسألَ مثل هذه الأسئلة في العراق وحذّرتُها: "ذلك قد يعرّضك للخطر ياايفا." تناولنا الغداء في فندق الرشيد وذلك كلّفَ آلاف الدنانير العراقية التي كادت قيمتها لاتساوي أكثر من بضعة مناديل ورقية. كانت مطبوعة على ورق رخيص هو نفسه الذي كانت تُطبع به المجلات المحلية بعد الحصار الاقتصادي الذي فُرض على البلد. دعوتُها الى البيت فطبختْ أمي لها أصنافاً من الطعام الشهي الممزوج بتوابل اعتادت أن تشتريها من سوق الشورجة. لكن ايفا أوقعتْ مزهرية قيّمة وكسرتْها فبكتْ. لم تعرف أمي التحدّث بالانكليزية لتهدئتها فأهدتْ لها، عوضاً عن الكلام، المزهرية الأخرى التوأم. ذهبْنا الى برج صدام الذي كان افتُتح توّاً. في الطابق العلوي الدوّار، نظرنا عبر النوافذ الى المدينة المدوّرة. بغداد بدتْ من فوق مدينةَ سلام، خضراء وجميلة. جلب النادل لنا قدحين من عصير البرتقال مجاناً حينما سمع بأن ايفا جاءت من السويد.

. . .

وضعتُ الرسائل كلها في كيس ورقي، كنتُ تسلمت بعضها بالبريد وبعضها باليد:
عيد سعيد!
هل وصلتك قبلاتي؟
يؤسفني أنَ أخبرك بأننا متوقفون عن نشر الشعر.
أحس كلما أردتُ كتابة رسالة بأنني سأترك شيئاً مني، ولم يتبق مني الكثير.
معذرة اذا لم أوفق في أن أحبكِ كما ينبغي.

أما زلت تحتفظين بقطعة النقد الايرانية القديمة؟

مازلتُ أحتفظ بالجريدة.

كتابك أول ديوان أقرؤه في حياتي فأنا لم أقرأ من قبل غير القصائد الموجودة في الكتب المدرسية.

ليسقط الثلج على رأسكِ انْ لم تأتي الى عمّان مرة أخرى.

عندما تدق أجراس الكنائس في الجمع الحزينة، اذكريني.

سأحبكِ حتى بعد الموت.

أتمنى لو أملك جهاز هاتف لأتصل بك.

هذه الرسالة شخصية جداً وأرجو ان لايطلع عليها بعد الله سواكِ.

بعد قليل لن نصبح غير أطياف شاحبة.

الاصدقاء الرائعون، كالأوطان، لايتكررون.

القصائد التي تكتبينها تفتقر الى الوزن والقافية ولكنها لاتخلو من ايقاع.

أنتِ مقدسة وخارجة على تشابه الرمال.

كل أمطار العالم لاتكفي لغسل لحظة حزن أصابتني منك.

مارسنا طقوس الغائب من أجلكِ.

هم متأخرون ولكننا في انتظارهم.

أخذ الكيسُ البلاستيكي يكبرُ في عمّان، بداخله الصور.

وضعتُ مشارقة أيضاً في الكيس. في احتفالية الوداع التي هيّأها لي في مكتب الجريدة، قال بأن مغادرتي لم تكن في صالح الجريدة وانما في صالح أميركا!

أضفتُ الى الكيس أيضاً صديقاً كان يعطيني كل شهر نسخة من مجلته "عمّان" ويقول: "ستضيعين في أميركا."

. . .

قطعنا الطريق الرملي الى البترا سيراً على الأقدام يتقدمنا آخرون فضلّوا أن يركبوا الحمير والجمال.

الغبارُ يتصاعد، يعلو ويهبط كأنفاسنا التي كادت تتقطع من التعب.

قبضة رمال وردية تحاول خنقي فأقطب جبيني.

آثار أقدام تتشكل وتختفي فوراً.

تخترقني نظرة وجه صخري مليء بالثقوب، نظرة صارمة ثابتة هكذا لاأدري منذ متى.

شقوق تكونت بفعل الانجراف خالقة أشكالاً بشرية بمختلف التعابير والملامح برغم

اشتراكها بذاك الثبوت الأزلي الرهيب.

استوقفني حجران بشريان متداخلان على نحوٍ من عناقٍ متكلس غريب، ولم تؤثر الانجرافات الخارجية الاّ في مسح المسافة الصخرية المستوية بينهما بتكوين، عوضاً عن ذلك، شقوق من الأيدي المتشابكة الى الأبد. أشكال صخرية أخرى تعدنا بنوع من اللااكتمال. لها جمالها الآخر السري لاتطرحه الاّ لعدد محدود من العابرين.

هناك جماجم فاغرة بلا أسنان توحي بهولٍ ما.

هذه الأجساد المنقوشة على الحجر ذات العيون المفتوحة الى الأبد، كان لها في الماضي رقصها وخمورها وحركتها الرشيقة، زلاتها، تذمراتها، ابتساماتها، دمعاتها، خيالاتها، سخافاتها، جمالاتها، ثرثراتها. والآن لها كل ذلك سوى اننا لانراه.

نتلمسُ النقوش التي تركتها الريحُ على الحجر، باتجاه شقٍ يعرف بـ " السيق". ندخلُ في الشق ونخرج منه مثل كائنات وُلدت تواً لتُترك في مواجهة غموض عظيم. ندخل ونخرج هكذا، بلا شيء، بلا يقين من شيء.

نسير في المضيق المؤدي الى "الخزنة." يُقال لاتُفتح الخزنة الا لمن يعرف سرها. ومن تُفتح له الخزنة تتحقق أمنيته تلك اللحظة.

حجارة ذات هيئة بشرية نحيفة أومأت لنا ايماءات رقيقة (ولو رصينة) ثم تقدمت وفتحت أمامنا كيساً من الجنفاص. عرفنا انه الكيس الذي سنضع فيه أمنياتنا التي قد تتحقق اذا فُتحت " الخزنة" لسبب أو لآخر.

تذكرتُ وأنا أنظر الى كيس ألامنيات، كيف كنت في فترة من فترات طفولتي انفقُ كل مالديّ لأسحب ورقة من كيس صغير في دكان شخص كنا ناديه بـ "عمّو." كنت أعطيه كل يوم خمسة فلوس، كانت هي كل ثروة الطفلة، في ذلك الوقت، مقابل أن أسحب ورقة من ذاك الكيس، اذ كان يزعم ان هناك أوراقًا رابحة بدمى حيوانات معروضة في دكانه.

كنت كل يوم أسحب ورقة مكتوب فيها "بوش" أي "لاشيء" بالعامية العراقية. وبعد أشهر طوال من فقدان يوميتي المالية في ذلك الكيس، قررتُ أن أحتال على "عمّو." كتبتُ في ورقة صغيرة كلمة "أرنب." طويتها وحشرتها في يدي. مددتُ يدي، بداخلها الورقة، ذلك اليوم، وأخرجتُها من الكيس لأواجههُ بكلمة "أرنب" بدلاً من "بوش." نظر الى الورقة مندهشاً وقال: "ولكن ليس عندي أي أرنب هنا في الدكان!"

. . .

في صور طفولتي، كل شيء بالأبيض والأسود:

على ظهر سفينة في نهر، كتبتُ قصيدتي الأولى. كانت عن موجات البحر التي تشبه حيواتنا ففي اللحظة التي تصل فيها موجة الى نهايتها، تكون موجة أخرى قد بدأتْ تواً .

ابن عمتي الذي كان معي في السفينة أخذ القصيدة وعمل منها زورقاً ورقياً ورماه في النهر، بينما بقينا ننظر الى القصيدة الزورقية وهي تبتعد.

هناك صورة لي وأنا أقرأ "مقبرة الأفيال" وهي أول قصة استهوتني، اذ تحكي كيف يذهب الفيل بنفسه الى مقبرته عندما يشعر بأنه سيموت. هكذا بكل بساطة، يضطجع على الأرض ويموت.

أمي، ببدلة العرس، تبدو أصغر من أبي بكثير. قالت لي: "ما رأيتُ أباك حتى ليلة الزفاف. ففي تلك الأيام كان الأزواج مثل سمك في النهر. فلاتعرفين ان كانوا صالحين أم طالحين. ولكن، الحمد لله، أبوك كان أحسن شخص في العالم."
في صور أخرى لها، كانت أمي ترتدي الكيمونو والتنورات القصيرة. "ذاك زمن الخير،" تقول.

مرة سهرتُ حتى الصباح في انتظار بابا نويل لأني صممت أن أراه شخصياً لا أن أتلقى هداياه المجردة. ظل أبي وأمي يترددان الى غرفتي لوضع هدية العيد تحت وسادتي ليجدانني مازلتُ مستيقظة. ولما أدركهما الصباح والتعب، أخبرانني بأنه ليس هناك بابا نويل. تلك كانت السنة التي أضعتُ فيها بابا نويل وهداياه أيضاً.

لي ضفيرة في صورتي مع ابن الجيران. مرة أعطاني رسالة مكتوب فيها: أنتِ طفلة ولاتفهمين في الحب.

هنا أبكي وأختبيءُ تحت السرير لأنهم قصوا ضفيرتي. أحدهم طبعَ قبلة خاطفة على فمي، وتصورتُ ذلك كافياً لأصبح حاملاً حتى اني تحسستُ بطني لأتأكد من ذلك.

وهناك مع جدتي، آكل الباقلاء وأفكر اني لابد ذاهبة الى الجنة اذ كانتْ تحكي لي عن مكان في الجنة محجوز لاولئك الذين يأكلون الباقلاء.

أمام الكاهن، أعترف بخطايا لم أرتكبها. كان لابد من ابتكار خطايا من أجل الاعتراف. نردد تراتيل بلهجة آرامية قديمة لم أفهمها. أهلي يتحدثون معي باللهجة الحديثة.

في الدير، ألتمس العزلة وأعود. كنتُ قررت أن أصبح راهبة لمجرد اني كنت أحتاج الى مكان خاص بي بعيداً عن الالتزامات العامة. لكني تراجعت عن قراري حين عرفتُ بأن

عليّ (كراهبة) أن التزم بزي موحد وأتبع قوانين صارمة.

لعبتُ الشطرنج في محاولة لتجسيد أفكاري وخططي على الرقعة من خلال أحجار(رموز) تتناوب في تشكيل احتمالات مع كل حركة، تقريباً مثل تشكيلات الشعر.

مثّلتُ العراق في بطولة شطرنج. جلستُ ساعات أمام الرقعة، قبل أن أرى تسرّب الوقت بين المربعات السود والبيض. في خضم الحروب، أعتزلتُ الشطرنج. كانت محض سخافة، أن تضحّي بكل اولئك البيادق من أجل حماية ملك واحد.

ضعتُ في أحد الأيام وأنا أعود من المدرسة الابتدائية الى البيت فدخلتُ الى الدكان الذي كان يرتادهُ جدي. سألتُ صاحب الدكان عن جدي فسألني فيما اذا كنتُ مسلمة أم مسيحية. لم أعرف الجواب. أراد أن يأخذني الى الجامع أو الى الكنيسة لكنني أردتُ أن يأخذني الى جدي. عثر عليّ جدي في الدكان واشترى لي علكة كالمعتاد.

في رفعة العلم، واقفة مع باقي الطالبات في ساحة المدرسة، نردّد النشيد الوطني: "وطنٌ مدّ على الأفق جناحا وارتدى ثوب الحضارات وشاحا..."
كانت معلمتي تلوم الاستعمار في كل شيء. سألتُها: "من هو الاستعمار؟" قالت: "ذلك معروف. بريطانيا."
في درس علم الأحياء، أشارت المعلمة الى صورة اميبيا قائلة: "هي خلية واحدة، لها عين وقدم وليس لها شكل محدَد. يمكن رسمها كما نشاء. في تلك اللحظة اكتشفتُ ماهو الشعر. هو اميبيا، له عين تشهد وقدم تترك آثاراً وشكل مرن.
ولكن في غرفتي، وأنا أعمل الواجب، لم أكتب سوى جملاً غير مفيدة.

هناك صور في الذاكرة، ماكان يمكن لأي كاميرا أن تصوّرها بكل شحناتها:
قلبي وهو يدق دقاته المدوية أمام الفراقات.
انفجارات هائلة وذبذبات بلا نهاية.
قارب يتأرجح لحظة مغادرة الركاب.
غصن يرتعش في عين طائر.
الجحيم تنبثق من كلمة.
الهواء وهو يغيّر مكان اقامته.
كرات تتقافز في الفضاء، هي مقطع عرضي من لحظة غضب.
فتاة مجنونة تطوف بكلب ميت.
قرد مضطرب في مختبر.

زجاج منثور في كل مكان.

. . .

من بين الرسائل كلها، رسالة واحدة أعدتُ قراءتها مرات ومرات، رسالة حب.
من بين الصور كلها، صورة واحدة بقيتُ أتأملها. نظهر فيها في الكلية، أنا ومازن مع
اثنين من أصدقائنا.

أروى وحسن عرّفا مازن اليّ في أثناء احدى اجازاته من معارك الفاو. كان قد قصّ
قصائدي من الصحف ورزمها معاً. أعطاني تلك الرسالة ونحن نسير تحت المطر من كلية
الآداب الى المكتبة المركزية في بغداد وهو يردد المقطع الأول من قصيدة "أنشودة
المطر" للسياب "عيناك غابتا نخيل ساعة السَحَر."

عندما غادرتُ البلد، لم أعرف أين كان مازن، ان كان حياً أم ميتاً. كانت صورته تشحب
مثل قمر قديم.

تخرّجَ من الكلية فاستدعي الى الجبهة مثل كل العراقيين المتخرجين. كان يحضر عادة
في الاجازات الى ساحة كلية الآداب فنلتقي مابين المحاضرات، وأحيانا أتغيب عن بعضها
وخاصة مادة "الثقافة القومية" المملة عن أيديولوجيا حزب البعث. كل مرة، أهيء له رزمة
من الكتب يأخذها معه الى الجبهة حيث الجيش يقاتل الايرانيين. في احدى تلك المرات،
حصلتُ على الكتب كلها في "شروة" واحدة من معرض بغداد الدولي للكتاب. في يوم
افتتاح المعرض، توافد الناس واحتشدوا أمام الباب منتظرين، وحين ضاق صبرهم بالباب
المسدود أمامهم، كسروه ودخلوا. في اليوم التالي، اقترح صحفيون تخصيص يوم لهم
وللأدباء لأنهم "يحتاجون الى الكتب أكثر من غيرهم" وانهم لم يتمكنوا من الوصول الى
الكتب بسبب الطوابير الهائلة الطويلة. لذلك قررت الحكومة تخصيص يوم من أيام
المعرض لكل مَن يحمل هوية اتحاد الأدباء أو الصحفيين. تمتعتُ ذاك اليوم بترف رؤية
الكتب كلها وملء عربتي بها. لافتات كثيرة كانت معروضة من أجل الدعاية ولكن واحدة
منها لاتخلو من صدق: "القاهرة تكتب، بيروت تنشر، بغداد تقرأ."
"القراءة أكثر النشاطات ترفاً في الجبهة"، قال لي مازن.

القناتان العراقيتان كانتا تبثان البرامج والأخبار نفسها تماماً، ولم نكن نعرف لماذا هما
قناتان اثنتان! كان برنامج "صور من المعركة" يبث يومياً مشاهد قتلى يغطيهم الرمل
والذباب وخوذات مبعثرة مع أعضاء بشرية. لم يكن بامكانك أن تميّز بين جثث العراقيين
والأيرانيين، فأجسادهم ممتزجة في تلك المنطقة الوسطى حيث الدم، الدم الأحمر نفسه،

يبقّع الجثث. ثم تشاهد أسرى المعركة، الأكثر حظاً تقريباً برغم مايبدون عليه من انهاك ووساخة. بعد ذلك، يمكنك أن تشاهد أفلام الكارتون وأشهرها توم وجيري.

كان مازن يحكي لي قصص الجنود. أحدهم خسر ساقيه فالتفتَ الى المضمّد يسأله فيما اذا كان عضوه التناسلي مازال على مايرام!
صديقهُ حسن يسألُ أسئلة مثل: كيف يمكن ألانحس بحركة الأرض؟
ماذا كان الله يفعل قبل أن يخلقنا؟
أيهما أهم: حريتك أم وطنك؟
هل تتناسب السعادة طرداً مع الغباء؟
ماالفرق بين الدموع في حالتي الألم والبصل؟
مامعنى يس – يم، يميناً يساراً؟
لانريد، يقرر حسن، أن نكون صوتاً في جوقة ولاقدماً من اقدام القطيع ولا خطوة في مشية عسكرية. يرى ان الموجات الصوتية التي تنبعث من النغمات الموسيقية على شكل نابض حلزوني ماهي الا الشكل نفسه الذي يتخذه وضع جسمهٍ في الجبهة. يستنتج أن صوت المدفع وصوت الموسيقى كليهما، للمفارقة، يؤديان الى توتر ينتج الشكل نفسه. الراحة، بالنسبة لحسن، لاتتحقق الا في النوم، لأن الوضع الأفقي هو الأفضل للانسان، فالوضع العمودي يسبب المشاكل. فمجرد الخروج الى الشارع يستدعي وضعاً عمودياً يعرّضه للانزعاج على أقل تقدير ان لم تكن ورطة أو حتى مأساة. لابد ان الله يحب الطيور حتى جعلها تتحرك بوضع أفقي. هناك، فوق، فوق الأشياء جميعاً.
في احدى المرات التي كان فيها حسن يسير في وضعه العمودي الاشكالوي، استوقفهُ أحد الذين يرتدون زياً موحداً وأخذهُ معهُ. بعد استجواب طويل، أرسلوه الى الجحيم فذهبَ. ذهبَ الى المكان الذي يصلح لزراعة العظام وتربية الجماجم، المكان المعبّأ في قنبلة موقوتة يمكن أن تنفجر في أي وقت. تلك اليمامة التي كانت قد حطّت على القنبلة، طارتْ، لحسن الحظ، في الوقت المناسب تماماً. عبثاً تحاول أروى تهدئته أو منعهُ من وضع يديه على أذنيه خشية انفجار ما. تتوق الى ذاك الوقت ماقبل الكارثة، وقت الكليّة بدون جبهة قتال.
مرةً زرنا معرضاً فنياً في مركز صدام للفنون:
أجنحة بلا طيور تنعكس في النهر
نظرة تنزلق وحيدة على زجاج نافذة
كولاج لساعة مقسومة الى نصفين على جدار مليء باعلانات من زمن آخر.
في قاعة أخرى لوحات فولكلورية لرجال بالكوفيات ونساء بالعبايات حول دلة قهوة كبيرة في خيمة شعَر سوداء، ولوحات خيول وقصب أهوار وسعف نخيل.

قاعة خاصة مكرّسة للوحات بورتريت لصدام بمختلف الأزياء والقبعات العسكرية والمدنية والعربية والكردية والخليجية، هنا يرتدي خوذة وهناك قبعة كاوبوي.

الحرب لامستْها ريشاتُ الفنانين بشكل مباشر وغير مباشر، بمختلف الأساليب السوريالية والتكعيبية والواقعية والتعبيرية والتجريدية.

في مقهى الخضراء، كنا نتحدث عن الكومبيوتر الذي بدأ يغيّر العالم ولكن ليس في العراق فلم يكن استخدامه مسموحاً بعد على صعيد الأفراد. كان حسن الأكثر اهتماماً بذلك فيخبر أروى بأنه في انتظار اليوم الذي يحلّ فيه الكومبيوتر محل الغباء البشري. الغباء الذي يلجأ الى الأسلحة، الغباء الذي يدعو الى الاصطفاف، الغباء الذي يصرخ من أجل لاشيء، الغباء الذي يحثّكَ لقتل شخص لاتعرفه ولم تره من قبل.

ولكن أروى تسأل: ماذا عن الانسان، فرحه، حزنه، احساسه؟

يجيبها حسن: بامكان الآلة أن تتوصل بمرور الوقت الى الاحساس بالأشياء تماماً مثل الانسان ناقصاً غباءَه وأنانيته وخبثه وحسده وكل نقاط ضعفه. ستتطور الآلة لتمثل طفولة الانسان الدائمة الذكاء. فلن تنشب حروب ولا كوارث ولن تكون هناك اهتمامات ايدلوجية مدمّرة ولابهلوانيات لغوية جوفاء ولانزاعات عدوانية.

- ولكن ألاترى ان الانسان، مع ذلك، يتفوق بالخيال؟ فلا يمكن للكومبيوتر، الذي يعارض مبدأ المصادفة، أن يرتاد المجهول أو ينجز اكتشافات عظيمة. فهل كان الكومبيوتر مثلا سيكتشف قانون الجاذبية بمجرد سقوط تفاحة على رأسهِ؟ وماذا عن الأحلام التي تميّز شخصاً عن آخر؟

- لن يكون هناك داعٍ للحلم، لأننا سنكون في الحلم. حلم مابعد الانسان حيث لا موت ولا ولادة.

- اذن كيف ستكون هناك حياة؟

- ستكون هناك حياة أخرى يعيشها الكائن الفائق الذي لايعرف شيئاً محدداً ولايرتبط بمصير معين ولايعترف بفكرة محددة واحدة.

- وماذا عن المتع الحسية البشرية؟

- سيقود التطور الالكتروني الى ابتكار بهجات غير تقليدية تتجاوز تلك الغرائز المستهلكة.

ستكون كل متعة قائمة بذاتها، لاتتكرر و لاتتأثر بالمؤثرات الخارجية. ستكون حياة صافية تماماً، بلا حكومات، بلا أعداء، بلا أحقاد، بلا انكسارات ولااحباطات مؤلمة، بلا أديان ولا أوثان، بلا نصر ولاخسارة.

- ذلك اذن عالم خالٍ من الفن، والا كيف يولد الفن في خضم هذا اللاشيء؟

- بل من هذا اللاشيء تحديداً يتحقق الفن خالصاً شفافاً. علينا أن نغادر هذه البقعة الى مكان آخر بلا حدود حيث ننبثق نقطتين مثل شمس وقمر. سنجعل الغيمة عربة لنا بلا مسارات محددة، نتبادل النجوم كلاماً، ونمطر من بعيد على الارضيين الذين لايرون أبعد من أنوفهم. سنرى الأرض بعين طائر.

دمَعَتْ عينا مازن وهو يتحدث عن موت حسن.
- "تناثرتْ جثتُهُ في الهواء أمام عيني. لفوا جثتهُ بالعلم العراقي وأخذوها الى أهله في زاخو"
- "هل تعرفْ أروى بذلك؟"، تساءلتُ.
- "لاأدري. كانت خيبته كبيرة عندما عاد من اجازته الأخيرة مرفوضاً من أهلها. ذهب طالباً يدها ولكن أباها قال بأنه لن يزوّج ابنته لكردي. اسمعي، سأهرب من الحرب، عبر الشمال، الى تركيا ومن ثمّ الى أي مكان آخر."
- "ماذا لو أمسكوا بك؟"
- " لايهمّني. كل يوم أشهدُ موتاً ما أو جرحاً أو غياباً. أفكرُ لو نتزوج بسرعة ثم يقوم شخص بتهريبنا عبر الحدود الى الخارج."
لكنني رفضت.

بعد بضعة أسابيع، شعرتُ بغلطتي.
غيابهُ شتتّ ذهني. وكانت أمسية اتحاد الأدباء، هذه المرة، باردة تماماً، فلم يكن مازن هناك ليحيّني كالمعتاد أو يبتسم لي. الهاتف مازال يرن ولكنه ليس في الطرف الآخر.
"يبدو انه يحبك فعلا"، علّقت لطفية عندما أريتُها رسالته.
هما لم يلتقيا يوماً، ولو كانا معاً في الكيس البلاستيكي.
بداخل كيس الصور، أصدقائي كلهم قريبون مني ومن بعضهم البعض مهما ابتعدنا في الواقع.

. . .

شهدتْ حديقة اتحاد الأدباء جدالات حادة بين الكتّاب وخاصة حينما كانوا يسكرون. أدباء الثمانينات اتهموا أدباء السبعينيات بالغموض واللامعنى. أدباء السبعينيات اتهموا أدباء الثمانينات بالمباشرة. كلا الجيلين اتفقا، على أية حال، بأن الأجيال السابقة لاتعرف بوجود أجيال لاحقة. الأجيال السابقة اتهمت اللاحقة بالتنكّر للآباء، وهكذا. ولكننا، من مختلف الأجيال، كنا نلتقي ليستمع أحدنا الى الآخر. تأخذ معك قصيدتك الأخيرة لأنهم يتوقعون منك شيئاً جديداً، وأنت بدورك تذهب لتستمع الى قصة أو قصيدة جديدة أو تشاهد لوحة أو تقرر أن تحضر فيلماً. كانت التعليقات التي تسمعها عادة مثل بندول يتأرجح بين طرفين. طرف يصيح "الله" بنبرة عالية مع "أعدْ، أعدْ"، وطرف يرى أن ترمي هذه الأوراق في سلة المهملات أو أن تشتغل على كتابتك أكثر. كان البندول نادراً مايستقرُّ في الوسط.

نصيف الناصري يمتدحك برسالة شعرية. يقول، عن مسألة الأجيال، بأن كل جيل يلغي الجيل الذي قبله مثلما يحدث مع "انقلاباتنا العسكرية الدموية" والسلطات التي تعاقبت على حكم العراق.

أطلق النقاد على جيلي الشعري اسم "جيل الحرب" وأحياناً "الشعراء الشباب." عدنان الصائغ ربما أول مَن أعلنَ عن ظهور جيلنا عبر ملف ثقافي بعنوان "انتبهوا رجاءً. الثمانينيون قادمون." قدّم به آراءنا نحن الذين كنا ننشر في فترة الثمانينات.

في يوم من الأيام، تحدّاني عدنان لأدخل معهم الى مقهى حسن عجمي الذي كان يرتاده الرجال من الأدباء. قالوا لي بأن أهم النقاشات والاكتشافات الأدبية كانت تطلع من ذلك المقهى. كنت المرأة الوحيدة معهم ذلك اليوم ولاأعرف اذا كانت هناك امرأة قبلي قد دخلت المقهى، انما لم أشعر بالأسف اني لم أدخله غير تلك المرة، فقد بدا لي كئيباً وغير مريح بالمرة. ماكنت سأحب أن أتحدث عن الشعر ولا عن أي موضوع آخر هناك. حتى الشاي الذي شربته لم يكن الأفضل. جلستُ بين عدنان وعبد الرزاق الربيعي. بعد دقيقة من جلوسي، تجاهلني الرجال في المقهى وعادوا الى نقاشاتهم ونرجيلاتهم ودوميناتهم ورقع الشطرنج وتسابيح الخرز ورميات النرد على رقع الطاولي. جاء النادل الذي كان يحمل بيديه ما بدا عشرة "استكانات" شاي ملتفتاً الى أحد الأدباء ليقول له بأنه لم يدفع الحساب في المرة الفائتة.

في يوم آخر، وأنا أحاول ايصال زوجة عدنان، ماجدة، الى بيتها، سرحتُ قليلاً فاستدرتُ بسيارتي الى القصر الجمهوري بينما كان المفترض التوجه الى أمام حيث نصب الحرية. جمدتْ قدمي على كابح السيارة حين رأينا أمامنا فجأة رجلين بملابس عسكرية موجهين بنادقهم الينا. لم ينزلا بنادقهم ولم يطلقا النيران بعد وقد مرّ قرن من الزمن فخمنتُ بأنهما مازالا يحاولان التصويب بدقة. أخيراً تقدّمَ أحدهما الى السيارة وأنا أفكر انه حتماً

لن يخطيء الهدف الآن من هذه المسافة القريبة. ولكنهُ قام بتفتيش السيارة ثم أشار نحو الاتجاه الذي يجب أن أتبعهُ خاتماً الكلام بعبارة "الله معك." فقدتُ في تلك اللحظة قدرتي على استيعاب ما أسمعهُ. كان قد أخذَ مني اجازة السوق ودوّنَ بعض الملاحظات وهو يستخدم قلمهُ بدلا من بندقيتِه، فحسب أحد الشعارات الحكومية "للقلم والبندقية فوهة واحدة."

عبد الرزاق فتح فمه الى أقصاه وهو يسمع قصة الضياع في القصر الجمهوري. هكذا يفعل دائماً اذ غالباً ما يندهش ثم يطلق ضحكة مدوية، انما من يعرفه جيداً يعرف بأنه شخص حزين. أخبرني ذات يوم بأن الحكومة أعدمت أخاه الذي رفض الالتحاق بالخدمة العسكرية. مُنعت عائلته من الحداد على القتيل وأُجبرت أن تدفع ثمن الطلقة التي استُخدمتْ في قتله. كنتُ أتذمر كلما أعطاني رزاق (كما نسميه) بطاقة باص. من كان يدري متى سيأتي الباص أو كم واحد سيصعد اليه أو يتعلق بمقبض الباب فلايترك مجالاً للداخل أو الخارج؟ ولكن رزاق قرر أن يشتري مليون بطاقة باص اذا ربح مليون دينار! كنا من بين مجموعة الشعراء "الشباب" الذين ذهبوا لمقابلة وزير الثقافة والاعلام آنذاك، حامد يوسف حمادي. دعانا الوزير بعد أن نُشرتْ قصائد لنا في ملف مجلة أسفار الشعري. رحّبَ بنا قائلاً: "كيف أحوال الشباب؟" ثم أخبرنا: "هذا الشعر الحديث الذي تكتبونه غير مفهوم بالمرة ولايخدم قضايانا المصيرية. لماذا ينبغي التحدث عن سلحفاة عندما يكون القصد التحدث عن الحرب؟ برأيي، كتابة قصيدة النثر تشبه الزواج من أجنبية."
وضعتُ يدي على فمي لأكتم ضحكتي أمام الوزير، ورزاق مرر لي ورقة عليها ملاحظة تقول بأن هذا يجعلهُ يرغب الزواج من أجنبية.
وقد تمّ له ذلك فعلاً. في عُمان، تزوّجَ من امرأة أمها بريطانية.

عدنان ورزاق تجدهما عادة معاً وأحياناً يلتحق بهما فضل خلف جبر. مرة خرجنا من منتدى الأدباء الشباب لنتغدى. كان مطعماً ذا رائحة زنخة مع كتل من اللحم الني معلقة أمامنا. انما كيف اختفى المطعم عن أنظارنا في اليوم التالي، لم نفهم. "ذاك المطعم الاسطوري"، سمّيناه.
حكى لي فضل عن مقلب صديقه جواد الحطاب الذي جاء اليه بعد منتصف الليل لأنه ضجر وأراد أن يتمشى فلم يمهله وقتاً ليغيّر ملابسه. وحين خرجا من مسكن فضل، أوقف جواد سيارة أجرة ليذهب بفضل الذي مازال ببيجامته الى ساحة التحرير في وسط المدينة. وهناك ابدى فضل تخوفهُ اذ وجد أمامه في الشارع مسؤولي انضباط مهتمين تفتيش هوية أي رجل في الطريق ليتأكدوا من سلامة موقفه من الخدمة العسكرية

فيقبضون بذلك على الفارين وعلى كل من لايحمل هوية، مهما كانت الأسباب. ارتعب فضل حين صرخ جواد قائلا أن صديقه لايحمل هوية! ولكن مسؤول الانضباط قابل صراخه بضحكة ومضى في طريقه.

قلت له: "ربما لم يشأ أن يضيع وقته مع مجنونين، واحد يصرخ وواحد بالبيجاما."

في الكيس البلاستيكي أيضا يوجد علي عبد الأمير الذي أشاركه حبه لفيروز، المغنية اللبنانية العظيمة. في الوقت الذي كانت فيه الصحف العراقية مليئة بصور المعركة وتكشيرات المسؤولين السياسيين ومواضيع تحذرك من "الاستعمار ومؤامرات الاعداء وقوى الشر والظلام" الخ، تطالعك مقالات علي عن غناء الريف الأمريكي وموسيقى الروك اندرول وفريق القمصان السود الغاضب. حضر علي في فندق الميليا منصور عرضهم الموسيقي (الروك) فكان الفريق، بقمصانه السود، يغني أغنية "ديفلز باراديس" أو جنة الشيطان، بايقاعات سريعة وصاخبة جداً. الجمهور، الذي كان أغلبه مرتدياً قمصاناً سوداً أيضاً، تفاعل مع تلك الايقاعات الى درجة صفق الكراسي، مما جعل ادارة الفندق تستدعي الشرطة وتوقف العرض. علي أوضح لي بأن تلك الحركات الصاخبة كانت في الحقيقة صرخات ضد الحرب المتواصلة في البلد. في الصورة، يظهر علي بملابس الخدمة العسكرية، بدلة خاكي وبسطال وخوذة. هو الذي، قبل ذلك بعشر سنوات، كان يسميه أصدقاؤه "هيبي" اذ كان يرتدي حذاءً كتانياً أبيض اللون ويكتب على حقيبته عبارة:
"Make love, not war"

من بين شعراء جيل الحرب أيضاً منذر عبد الحر. كان يسميني "أختي." أتذكرهُ يذهب باحثاً في الحانات عن جان دمو، الشاعر العظيم بسهوه. لم يزاول جان عملاً ولم يمتلك الكثير من القصائد فقد كان يبيع قسماً منها لشعراء يملكون المال ولكن ينقصهم الالهام. القصائد المتبقية له جُمعَت في ديوان وحيد بعنوان "الأسمال." في أثناء الحرب العراقية الايرانية في الثمانينات، أُخذ جان من الحانة الى الجيش. أعطوه مهمة حارس ليلي. كان جان ينام في الأوقات غير المناسبة. حذّرهُ الضابط قائلا: "جان، أنت جندي ولايجوز لك أن تنام وقتما تشاء." قال جان: "لماذا؟" فتساءل الضابط: "تقصد لماذا لايجوز أن تنام؟" أجاب جان: "لا. لماذا أنا جندي؟"

كان جان معروفاً بضحكته الساخرة التي كان يطلقها كلما استمع الى قصيدة عمودية أو "تعبوية." كنا ننظر الى ممارسات وتعبويات "الحزب والثورة" بوصفها نكتة. انما لم يكن منا، سوى جان دمو، مَن يجرؤ أن يضحك وقتما يشاء وأينما يشاء من تلك النكتة. لم نكن نضحك من واقع الحال الا في أماكن خاصة مع أصدقاء موثوق بهم، بمعنى انهم لن يكتبوا عنك تقريراً يؤدي بك الى الجحيم على أقل تقدير.

احتشد الجمهور في اتحاد الأدباء لحضور الأمسية الشعرية التي أُقيمتْ لجان لكنهُ لابد
نسي كعادته. وبعد أن أتوا به أخيراً من الحانة وأجلسوه في المكان المخصص، وقفَ
جان ليلقي بضعة أسطر ثم جلسَ وانتهى من مهمّته فهو لايحب أن يقرأ. كانت تلك أمسيته
الوحيدة تحدّثَ فيها نقادٌ حلّلوا شعره وحداثته وهو سارح عنهم في عوالمه الأخرى.
بلا مأوى كالعادة، عُثر على جان ميتاً على قارعة طريق في أستراليا.

مثل جان دمو، يوسف الصائغ كان أقرب الى الشعراء الشباب مما هو الى شعراء جيله،
أو هكذا بدا لي على الأقل. كان يوسف شاعراً حقيقياً برغم انتمائه الى حزب البعث. أجلّ
مرةً موعداً مهماً له مع مسؤولين حكوميين ليحضر احدى قراءاتنا الشعرية. في اليوم الذي
كنتُ فيه ذاهبة لتسليم مخطوطة كتابي "مزامير الغياب" لمطبعة الأديب البغدادية، التقيتُ
بيوسف مصادفة عند مصعد وزارة الثقافة والأعلام وقد بدا لي مثل نويل بابا بلحيته
البيضاء. سألني عن أخباري الشعرية فأخبرتهُ عن المخطوطة وعن نية المصمم أن يصحب
القصائد بتخطيطات، فكانت تلك "موضة" سائدة في دواوين الشعر. "مَن سيعمل
التخطيطات؟" سأل يوسف. "لاأدري بعد"، قلتُ لهُ. "تعالي نعالج هذا الأمر" اقترحَ في
الطريق الى مكتبه في دائرة السينما والمسرح الذي كان هو مديرها العام. "ما رأيكِ بعلاء
بشير؟" سألني. قلتُ له: "د. علاء بشير فنان عظيم ولكن انه لابد انه مشغول جداً." كان
جراحاً معروفاً وطبيباً خاصاً لصدام، تحتاج الى أشهر لحجز موعد معه.
رفع يوسف سماعة الهاتف وتحدّثَ مع الدكتور. جاء، لدهشتي، بعد دقائق ربما مثلما يفعل
حينما يُستدعى الى جريح في غرفة طوارئ. فهمتُ بأنهما صديقان حميمان وانه كان
سيأتي لزيارته على أية حال. صافحني د. بشير وجلس. ملامح وجهه بارزة مثل نحت.
شعره طويل من الخلف ولكن ليس له شعر من الأمام. بادره يوسف بالقول: "أنت تعرف
هذه الشاعرة. أليس كذلك؟ أريد منكَ أن تعمل تخطيطات لبعض قصائدها. مارأيك؟" أومأ
د. بشير برأسه مبتسماً. أعطاه يوسف بعض قصائدي في ملف ثم عاد الى موضوع فيلم
"رجل المطر" الذي كنا نتحدث به والذي كان قد عُرض في نادي السينما. أخذ د. بشير
يتصفح القصائد بهدوء ثم بدأ يشتغل بقلم رصاص. تمنيتُ، في أثناء ذلك، لو تبتلعني
الأرض فأختفي عن أنظار الدكتور الذي استُدعي الى قصائدي بهذه الطريقة الطوارئية.
ولكنه، بعد فترة قصيرة، وضعَ التخطيطات على الطاولة طالباً أن نحزر أي قصيدة تمثّل
كل منها. بدأ يوسف قبلي: "لابد ان هذه عن المرأة التي تشكو من صداع. هذه عن
الحرب".
في يوم آخر، حينما جلبتُ ليوسف نسخته المطبوعة تواً من ديواني، عرّفني الى زوجته
الجديدة. نزع حجابها ليريني كيف انه حلق لها شعرها بأكمله. فكرتُ "لابد انها مجنونة
مثله."

كانت زوجة يوسف الأولى قد ماتت بحادث سيارة وقد تدحرجت تفاحاتها معها من السيارة. أصدرَ يوسف ديواناً عنها بعنوان "سيدة التفاحات الأربع."

عندما صدر كتابي "مزامير الغياب"، اتصل بي المخرج المسرحي د. صلاح القصب الذي كان معروفاً بمسرح الصورة التجريبي. قال لي ان مسرحيته الجديدة مستلهمة من قصائدي فدعاني الى حضورها. لم أستطع ربط المشاهد بقصائدي، ولكن أسعدني تحمّسهُ لتلك "الصور الشعرية." احتوتْ معظم المشاهد على بانيوات ودراجات بخارية وشخوص يرتدون كلهم نظارات شمسية. كان أحد طلابه في أكاديمية الفنون الجميلة قد أخبرني بأن د. القصب مهووس بالنظارات الشمسية وانه يرتديها كل يوم. كنتُ في البيت مع أمي ننزل الملابس من السطح بعد أن انتهت الشمس من تجفيفها وكويها على الحبال عندما أرسلَ لي د. القصب بيانو بلا مناسبة. كان متروكاً في المسرح للغبار والأوراق المكدّسة. قال: "أنا واثق بأنك تعرفين قيمتهُ."
كان بيانو ضخماً بالكاد حملهُ الرجال الى تلك الزاوية في غرفة المعيشة. لم تحب أمي مكانهُ ولكنه أثقل من أن يُزاح لذلك مكث هناك ربما الى الأبد.

. . .

حملتُ كوبين من الشاي الى الحديقة حيث خالد م. يجري معي لقاءً صحفياً وفي الخلفية زهور الرازقي البيضاء. سألني عن استخدامي للشطرنج والهندسة في الشعر وعن الحائط الذي يفصل حديقتنا عن حديقة الجيران اذ كان قد سقط بأكمله فجأة كتلة واحدة. أخبرتهُ بأني واخواني الأربعة عادة نجلس هنا مساء وبنات الجيران يجلسن هناك وراء الجدار (قبل سقوطه) ولكن الحمد لله سقط ونحن نيام دامجاً الحديقتين الى واحدة. تركناه هكذا لنشترك نحن والجيران بهذه الأرض في الأمسيات التي تمتدّ أحياناً الى منتصف الليل، بل ونشترك بالمقبلات والمشروبات حول المائدة.

كنا نتبع الارشادات بترك مكاتبنا التابعة لوزارة الثقافة والاعلام لحضور قراءات شعرية رسمية في قاعات ذات أبواب يحرسها رجال شرطة لايسمحون لك بالمغادرة قبل انتهاء القراءة. منها قصائد تعبوية أو ممجّدة لصدام أو للجيش ومنها قصائد غزل تستجيب لها بتنهيدة مثل استراحة محارب، قصائد عمودية وفق بحور الشعر الستة العشر التي أوجدها الخليل بن أحمد الفراهيدي في القرن الثاني للهجرة.
ولكن خالد كان دائماً يَتمكن من ايجاد طريقة للخروج. آخر الخروجات التي ساعدني فيها خالد كان خروجاً من العراق. لم أفكر أبداً بالشعر كمهنة، انما ذلك ما فكر فيه خالد.

أقنعَ موظفَ الجوازات بأن يدوّن في جوازي: المهنة الحالية لحاملة الجواز هي "شاعرة."

. . .

لم تتوفر لي فرصة قراءة كل تلك الكتب على الرفوف. طلبتُ من لطفية أن تحتفظ ببعضها وسيذهب المتبقي الى مستودع أبن خالتي حتى أتمكن لاحقاً من استعادتها حينما أعود الى البلد. كانت الكتب الممنوعة متوفرة أيضاً اذ يجري تهريبها الى الداخل، مغلفةً بأغلفة كتب أخرى. حسين الحسيني يعثر على أي كتاب تفكر به ويجلبه لك ضاحكاً. بل انهُ يحصل لك على سجائر أو يساعدك في الخروج من سجن. كان يعرف الوزراء كلهم واحداً واحداً ودلة القهوة التركية دائماً ساخنة في مكتبه. كانت رائحة القهوة ماتزال هناك بعد دخوله السجن. عُفي عنه فخرج وهو يشتم ويطلق نكاته الساخرة. مرةً اتصل بمدير عام في الوزارة مخاطباً اياه: "كيف حالك يا ناطور؟" وذلك بعد خطاب لصدام واصفاً مسؤولي الدولة بالنواطير. بعد أن غادرتُ العراق، طلبت الحكومة من أخي أن يدفع نفقات دراستي الجامعية. بعثتُ له رسالة لأن يأخذ معهُ الحسيني الى الوزارة تحسباً لأية مضايقة.

كان المتوقع منا أن نتبع الارشادات وأن نقلق.
النقاد فقط كان يمكن تجاهلهم دونما قلق. بعد كل حرب، يقدمون نظرياتهم عن أدب مابعد الحرب. ولكن مَن يبالي؟ لم يكن هناك أدب مابعد الحرب في العراق أبداً.
جيل الحرب الثمانيني تُبع بأجيال حرب أخرى.
ولكن قيل ان جيلنا تميز بظهور شاعرات عددهن، ولو أقل من أصابع يد واحدة، كبير بالقياس الى الأجيال الأخرى.
من بين شاعرات جيلي، سهام جبار بدت لي الأكثر حداثة وجرأة في الكتابة ولو الأكثر تقليدية في المظهر، اذ ترتدي الحجاب. ولكن مزقّ أهلُها كتبَها لئلا "تضيّع وقتها في قراءات فاسدة بدل أن تساعد في شغل البيت وتنتهيَ للزواج."

بالعكس من ذلك، ريم قيس كبة محافظة شعرياً ولكن عصرية المظهر. أهلها بمنتهى اللطف والترحيب. كان بيتهم من طراز شارع "أبو نؤاس" على نهر دجلة مع نخلة كبيرة تتوسط الصالة. لم يكن مسموحاً للنساء بالدخول الى مقاهي حدائق "أبو نؤاس" (التي كانت تفوح منها رائحة السمك "المسكوف" اللذيذ) الا برفقة رجالهن. فكنتُ أجد في جلساتي في منزل ريم بعض التعويض اذ كنا غالباً مانأخذ راحتنا هناك في التهكم على ممارسات الحكومة والتحدث عن واقع البلد السوريالي، اذ كان النهر الكبير أمامنا يفصلنا

عن اي جدران "قد تكون لها آذان."

أما أمل الجبوري فكانت تتذمر لأنه "لاأحد يعترف لها بجميل."
حينما تخرّجنا من الجامعة، ساعدتْني في تغيير وظيفتي. رافقتني الى وزارة التخطيط
لتقوم "بالوساطة" لي. كنتُ قد استدعيت للعمل كمدرّسة لغة انكليزية، وذلك حسب التعيين
المركزي، اذ تذهب لتعثر على اسمك في لوحة كبيرة ومعه وظيفتك المقررة. لم تكن لي
رغبة على الاطلاق بأن أشتغل في التدريس. كنت نويت، منذ الطفولة، أن أصبح صحفية.
أهلي، من ناحية أخرى، توقعوا أن أتخصص بالرياضيات أو الهندسة. كنتُ دائماً أساعد
الطالبات في مادة الرياضيات بعد انتهاء الدوام. ولأني كنتُ أسوأ مدرّسة في العالم، كنت
أفتقر الى الصبر وأرفض الاعادة أكثر من مرة واحدة، فتضطر الطالبات أخيراً الى نقل
الأجوبة، بينما أمي تعترض قائلة: "لا تكوني لئيمة."
مسؤول التخطيط الذي كانت تعرفهُ أمل أخذ منا الأوراق الرسمية وطلب لنا شاياً. وقبل أن
نكمل احتساء الشاي، غيّر الرجل مهمتي الوظيفية اذ نقلني من وزارة التربية الى وزارة
الثقافة والاعلام. خرجتُ وأنا أتنفس الصعداء وكأني سمعتُ قاضياً يعلن براءتي ويطلق
سراحي. تذمرتْ أمل هذه المرة بأني أستاذة شطرنج ماهرة ولكن لا أتذكر الطريق الى
بيتها.

كنتُ أحياناً ألتقي بلطفية الدليمي خارج المجموع لنتحدث عن أمورنا الشخصية أو
"نقشب" عن باقي الأدباء أو ننتقد الحكومة أو نشرب شاي الساعة الخامسة بالنعناع.
كانت من جيل آخر. كلما ودّعتُها ذكّرتني أن أتجنب الطرق السريعة وأن أقرأ "ضرورة
الفن" لارنست فيشر. كانت تتوق دائماً لمحبٍ مثل بطل قصة قرأَتْها، يفاجيء حبيبته بأن
يعبيء غرفة الفندق بالبرتقال فتتمرغ البطلة بتلك الفاكهة حالما تدخل الغرفة.
تقول لي: "الحياة جميلة، ألاتظنين؟"
أقول: "أظنها جميلة ان شئنا ذلك."
– "اللحظة الحاضرة وحدها هي التي تهم. اللحظة هي الحقيقة، الآن هو الزمن. "

اللحظة؟ أين هي اللحظة؟ اننا لانلبث أن ننطقها أو نفكر فيها حتى تنتهي وتعطي مكانها
للحظة أخرى فسرعان ما تصبح ماضياً. العالم فعل ماضٍ توّاً.

كانتْ لطفية تبكي كلما تذكرت ولديها اللذين رحلا الى اوربا. نصف الناس الذين عرفتْهم
رحلوا. النصف الآخر يستعد للرحيل. "لمن تُترك هذه المدينة اذن؟ مَن سيرمّم الجمال
النائم فيها تحت الأنقاض؟" تتساءل.

"أدباء الخارج" و "أدباء الداخل" من المصطلحات الجديدة التي دخلت الصحافة ولكنهم باتوا يخرجون واحداً بعد الآخر ويكتبون عن الداخل من بعيد، من الخارج.

. . .

في عيد ميلادي الواحد والثلاثين، أخذتْني الطائرة الى الأرض الجديدة. كولمبس وصل الى أميركا لأن العالم كان دائرياً. أنا وصلتُ بعده بحوالي ٥٠٠ سنة لأن العالم أصبح مربعاً وأردتُ أن أختبئ في احدى الزوايا.

كانت الغيوم، كما هي دائماً، قطنية شفافة قريبة بعيدة مثل حلم. قررتُ الادعاء بأنني لا أعرفُ التحدث بالانكليزية حتى أتجنبَ الحديث مع جارتي في الرحلة. أخشى انه من غير المناسب القول بأنني عراقية ومن الصعب العثور على جملة مفيدة اذا سألَتْني لماذا أذهب وماذا سأفعل في أميركا. ولكن لم تبادرني الجارة بالكلام. لم تسألني عن حرب الخليج الأولى ولا الثانية ولم تتحدث حتى عن المناخ. كانت تتصرف بيسر مع الموجودات وكنتُ أقلدها في استخدام الحاجيات وخاصة تلك الالكترونية منها التي فاجأتني بوجودها تحت المقعد وبجانبه. كنت راكبة في مقصورة من الدرجة الاولى مخصصة عادة للأشخاص المهمين جداً. حدث ذلك بسبب غلطة حيث فوجئتُ في مطارامستردام بقولهم اني لا أملك فعلياً بطاقة من امستردام الى ديترويت، انما من عمّان الى امستردام فقط! وحين أكدتُ باني كنتُ قد دفعتُ حق البطاقة كاملة وانهم لابد أن يسمحوا لي الآن بالصعود الى الطائرة فأنا لا أعرف أحداً في امستردام ولا أعرف ماذا أفعلُ فيها، أعطوني المقعد الوحيد المتبقي في الطائرة وكان في مقصورة الدرجة الاولى. طبعاً لم أمانع تلك الغلطة التي وضعتني مع رجال ونساء الأعمال الذين بالتأكيد لم يذهبوا يوماً الى سوق مريدي في بغداد حيث تعثر على حاجتك المسروقة لتشتريها من جديد بأسعار مضاعفة! هكذا أصبحتُ، لساعات، شخصية مهمة جداً تقابَلُ بحفاوة من التحيات والابتسامات وتتفرج على شاشة تلفاز بمنتهى الصغر وتأكل حبات الفستق وتحتسي نبيذاً أحمر. تلك الأشياء أيضاً جاءتني بالغلط.

انسكبَ النبيذ على ملابسي وتذكرت أمي التي تُعزي كل الأشياء التي تنسكب الى "خير" أو "شر." فالسكّر مثلاً خير اذا تناثر والملح شر اذا وقع وانكسر وانكسار سيُهزَمُ الشر واذا وقع ولم ينكسر ذلك سيء، والقهوة اذا انسكبت على ملابسك فيعتمد الأمر فيما اذا كانت حلوة أم مرة. لم أستطع أن أتذكر أحكامها بخصوص النبيذ.

انتابني خوفٌ من اهتزازٍ مفاجيء للطائرة. وجدتُ الركاب المهمين جداً مندمجين في القراءة أو النوم فقلّدتُ هدوءهم وأزحت الخوفَ جانباً. بعد فترة التسعة أشهر التي أمضيتُها في عمّان، لابد أن جنيناً ما قد تهيأ الآن للخروج الى العالم. بدأتُ بمراجعة بعض مسودات قصائدي التي كتبتُها في الأردن، منها ثمانية وعشرون قصيدة مكرّسة للحروف العربية حيث تبدأ كلمات كل قصيدة منها بأحد تلك الحروف. استغربتُ من نفسي ولم أفهم ما الذي دعاني الى الكتابة على تلك الشاكلة.

هبطت الطائرة الى ديترويت والمضيفةُ تمنتْ لي يوماً سعيداً. لم تكن مسألة يوم بالنسبة لي، كنتُ على وشك أن أخبرها.

في المطار، أخذوني جانباً في غرفة مع شرطية سألتْني الكثير من الأسئلة وهي تنظر بريبة الى جواز سفري وكأنها تتساءل عن كيفية منح تأشيرة "سائحة" لواحدة قادمة من تحت الأنقاض. أخذوا بصمات أصابعي عدة مرات والتقطوا لي صوراً كثيرة . لم أكن متأكدة فيما إذا كان المفروض أن أبتسم ولم أعرف ان كانوا يظنونني شاعرة مشهورة أم مجرمة.

أخيراً ختمتْ الشرطيةُ جوازي. وتلك كانت غلطة أخرى. ختمتْ "أيار ١٩٩٧" بدلاً من "١٩٩٦." فأعطتني سنة وثلاثة أشهر بدلاً من ثلاثة أشهر. ربما أعجبتْها بصمات أصابعي التي ياما استُخدمتْ لحمل الأقلام ومسح الدموع، ولكنها في المستقبل، عندما أعود الى العراق، ستُستخدم لتغطية عيون أصدقائي حتى يحزروا مَن في الخلف. ذهبتُ لالتقاط حقيبتي التي كانت قد تُركت وحيدة تدور هناك كأنها تبادلني الحيرة.

لوري، محامية الهجرة، هي التي لاحظت الغلطة في جواز سفري.
وهي أول أمريكية تنضم الى كيس الصور البلاستيكي.
كان يمكن اضافة اسم مازن الى استمارتي لطلب اللجوء اذا كان حياً. كنتُ بحثتُ عن اسمه في قوائم أسرى الحرب لكنه لم يكن هناك ولا في أي قائمة أخرى. كان المفترض بكلمةِ "حي" أن تترك آثاراً ولم يكن عندي أثر غير صورتنا في جامعة بغداد، تلك الصورة الشاحبة كالقمر. أما أثر لمسته لِيدي فلم يمكن تبيّنه ولا ازالته.
لوري هي التي أرتني نصب الحرية لأول مرة في حياتي. أشارتْ لاحقاً الى المكان الفارغ الذي كان قد احتله سابقاً برجا مركز التجارة العالمي. تخيلتُ تلك الأجساد تتعثرُ من فوق الى الأسفل والأحاديث مبتورة في منتصف حيواتهم.
تحدثتُ الى لوري عن دائرة رقابة المطبوعات في العراق. بداخل تلك البناية، كان يشتغل

موظفون من مهامهم حماية "الأخلاق العامة" وحذف المقاطع "غير المناسبة" أخلاقياً أو فكرياً. هم الذين يمنحونك ورقة تصديق قبل أن تطبع كتابك. ورقة التصديق، على أية حال، لاتعني انك حتماً بمنأى عن الخطر. الرقيب الآخر المتطوع الذي ظنوا بأنهم دربوه جيداً هو أنت. اختفاء بعض الأدباء عن الأنظار مثلاً كفيل بالقيام بذاك التدريب. سألني أحدهم عن نص "يوميات موجة خارج البحر" وماهو القصد من وراء شخصية "زيوس"؟ أجبتُ بانها "ليست مهمة الكاتب تفسير النص. تلك مهمة القاريء."

مرة بعثتْ لي دار الجمل في ألمانيا ثلاثة كتب ممنوعة. حضر شخصان الى مكتب رئيس تحرير جريدة بغداد اوبزرفر التي كنت أعمل فيها وسألاني فيما اذا طلبتُ تلك الكتب. قلت "لا." قال أحدهما "أ تريدين هذه الكتب؟" أجبتُ، "لا." وأخيراً خرجا بالكتب، من دوني!

مديري ذاك (ن. الحديثي)، وهو رجل دمث، تنهّدَ بارتياح. كان من المديرين القلائل الذين لم يربوا شوارب، ولو اني رأيته مرة بشارب في التلفزيون حين أصبح وزيراً للخارجية. كان صدام قد أمر مسؤولي الدولة بتربية شواربهم وبتخفيف أوزانهم.

في بنايتنا القديمة الحميمة دار الجماهير، كنا نضع المواضيع في سلة خيزران صغيرة مربوطة بحبل ننزله من الطابق الثاني الى الأول ليتسلمها موظفون آخرون يقومون بطبع المواد وتنضيدها ولصقها وايجاد صور تتماشى معها. كانت جريدتنا تخرج يومياً بتصميم لايختلف عن الجرائد الأخرى: في الصفحة الأولى صورة "الرئيس القائد" ونشاطاته، وفوق في الزاوية عبارة تدعوك لأن تكتب "دونما خوف أو تردد سواءً كانت الدولة راضية أم غير راضية." تلك كانت للديكور فقط. لم تكن هناك ساعة غداء أو استراحة محددة، فنصعد الى الكافيتريا في الطابق الثالث كلما جعنا أو مللنا أو أردنا التحدث بأي شأن ماعدا السياسة. مرة سألتُ عن حسن مطلك اذ كان قد أهدى اليّ رواية مع توقيع وعبارة لها علاقة بلعبة الشطرنج. همسوا لي بأنه اختفى. "لا تسألي"، قالوا.

كنا نقدم المواد بخط اليد أو مطبوعة ببطء على الآلة الكاتبة. كانت مواضيعي غالباً مليئة بأسهم تؤدي الى اسطر مائلة وحلزونية، ليس مثل مواضيع صديقتي هدى التي كانت تعيد الطباعة كلما أخطأت. كنا نعتمد على تقارير وكالة رويترز البريطانية فلم نكن نشطب منها سوى الجمل أو الفقرات التي تخالف كلام "قيادتنا الحكيمة." فكان لابد مثلاً من ابدال عبارة "غزو العراق للكويت" بعبارة "ضم العراق للكويت." كنت أحياناً أسهو عن مثل تلك التعديلات فيعدّلها مدير التحرير "أبو ايمان." لاأنسى مزاحه حين سُئل، وهو كردي، فيما اذا كان يساند "الطلباني" أم "البرزاني"، فأجاب بأنه يساند "الطرزاني." أما تغيير مواد "الأشوسييتد بريس" من الانكليزية الأمريكية الى الانكليزية البريطانية، فبرّره بنكتة:

تشاجرَ امريكي وبريطاني حول تسمية المصعد بـ "أليفيتر" أو "لفت." فقال الأمريكي: "نحن الذين اخترعنا المصعد ومن حقنا تسميته مانشاء." فأجاب البريطاني: "ولكننا اخترعنا اللغة الانكليزية ومن حقنا تسميته مانشاء."

بعد العمل، كنتُ أذهب أحياناً مع هدى الى "شارع النهر" حيث نتبادل الأسرار. وأحياناً تأتي معنا بقية صحفيات الجريدة (اسراء و بان) فنسمع أحاديث ممتعة مثل قفل العباس لتحقيق الأمنيات. كان المفترض باحداهن أن تعود لفتح القفل حتى تتحقق أمنيتها ولكنها نسيت ولم يعد الأمر يجدي لأن حبيبها تزوج ابنة عمه.

· · ·

لوري كبستْ مع وثائق اللجوء موضوعاً صحفياً في جريدة عراقية. يورد الخبر أسماء كتاب عراقيين تركوا البلد لانهم "خونة." كان اسمي في القائمة وبجانب اسمي "أميركا" مكاناً للاقامة.

المرة الأولى التي أردتُ فيها أن أسافر الى أميركا كانت في عام ١٩٨٣ لأسباب مختلفة جداً.

كنتُ دائماً متفوقة في مادة الرياضيات فقرّرَ أبي ارسالي الى أميركا للدراسة على نفقته الخاصة حتى أُعرّف العالم على "اختراعاتي في الرياضيات." أرسلَ لي عمي، الذي كان يعيش في ديترويت، قبولاً من جامعة وين ستيت. كان من ضمن المتطلبات أن آخذ كورساً في اللغة الانكليزية بكلفة أحد عشر ألف دولار في السنة بضمنها المعيشة. "لامشكلة في ذلك"، قال أبي "فالدينار العراقي يساوي ثلاثة دولارات."

أخبرتُ الجميع بأنني سأسافر للدراسة في الخارج. تحدثتُ عن الموضوع اثنتي عشرة ساعة في النهار، وأمضيتُ النصف الآخر من اليوم في التفكير بالتفاصيل: العيش مستقلة وحدي في شقة، أقرأ ماأشاء حتى الكتب الممنوعة، لا ضيوف كثر، لازواجات مدبّرة من الأقارب، لاشفقة على عزلتي مع الكتب. سأذهب آلاف الأميال بعيداً عن الحرب وأصوات الغارات والانفجارات، عن أدب المزبلة التعبوي، عن الصواريخ العراقية والأيرانية التي كانت تنطلق باتجاهين متعاكسين، عن برامج محطتي التلفزيون، عن لافتات الشوارع التي تذكّرك كل يوم بان "كل عراقي هو مشروع استشهاد" و"كل العراقيين بعثيون وان لم ينتموا،" بعيداً عن كل ذاك الزجاج المكسور مابين الأجنحة الملونة في حلم دودة القز.

أخبرتُ ابنة الجيران، التي كانت تتأرجح معي في الحديقة، خطوة الى الأمام وأخرى الى الخلف، كيف سأذهب في اليوم التالي الى وزارة الخارجية للحصول على موافقة بالسفر. قالت أمي، "الناس مجانين في أميركا، فهم يربون القطط والكلاب في بيوتهم."

كل ذلك تلاشى.
"حسب القانون الجديد، لا يجوز للمرأة العراقية أن تسافر للدراسة على النفقة الخاصة وقت الحرب."
قال أبي لابد أنّ هذا قانون استثنائي في وقت استثنائي، أغلب الظن سيُلغى بعد انتهاء الحرب.
واقترحَ أن أدرس الأدب الأنكليزي في بغداد حتى أكون جاهزة حين يتبدّل القانون.

. . .

في ساحة كلية الآداب، كنا نناقش مسرحيات شكسبير ونأكل الحمص من العربات المتجولة وأحيائاً نتمشى الى المعهد البريطاني حيث نستعير كتباً باللغة الانكليزية وأفلاماً أجنبية أو نحتسي شاياً أو قهوة في حديقة المعهد الرائعة التي يتفيء العشاق عادةً تحت ظلال أشجارها.
كنا نتأبط الكتب والأفلام والمحاضرات الى المسيرات الطلابية التي كنا نساق اليها بمناسبة وبدون مناسبة. ماكان من الحكمة أن تمانع أو حتى تسألْ ففي نهاية الأمر ستسمع "نفّذْ ثم ناقشْ." ولكننا حوّلنا تلك المسيرات الى مناسبات للمشي ومناقشات في الثقافة والفن ومسرحيات عوني كرومي وموسيقى نصير شمة ولوحات ستار كاووش وجواربه الحمراء. لم يكن أي منا يعير انتباهاً الى صراخ طلاب الاتحاد في المقدّمة.

كنت مشغولة بما يكفي لأن أنسى أميركا. ورقة القبول من جامعة "وين ستيت" تركتُها في جارور مع قصائد لم أجرأ على نشرها و دفتر قديم فيه رسومات من المرحلة الأبتدائية.

عندما تخرجتُ، لم يتغير القانون فلم أستطع الذهاب الى أميركا. لكن بعد حين، دعتني غادة، وهي رسامة صماء، الى مرافقتها كمترجمة. كنتُ أتحدث الى غادة بالكتابة في دفترها وكانتْ أحياناً تستخدم صوتها الواطيء المتقطع. مرة دعوتُها الى قراءة شعرية لي ناسية انها لن تتمكن من أنْ تسمع شيئاً. جلستْ في الصمت وهي تبتسم. غادة رسمتْ مرة وزير الدفاع وأهدتُ اللوحة، فكافأها بأن قرّرَ ارسالها للعلاج في الخارج على نفقته الخاصة. وأنا كنتُ قد ملأتُ دفترها بانتقادات لأدب الحرب في العراق لأن أغلبه يتحدث

عن بطولات مقيتة ويصوّر الجندي العراقي كسوبرمان وليس كإنسان، وعن "أنواط شجاعة" تُعطى يومياً للجينرالات والقتلة، وجوائز تُمنَح للكتّاب والفنانين الذين يمتدحون القتل. أردتُ أن أطلب منها تلك اللحظة ألا تُري دفترها للوزير ولكني لم أفعل. قالتْ، "ابن القحبة، كان لابد أن أرسمهُ." ثم دعتني أن أرافقها كمترجمة لأن المكرمة تتضمن مرافقة.

في دائرة الجوازات، نقلتُ قولهم الى دفتر غادة بأن عليها أن تأخذ معها أحد أفراد عائلتها وليس واحدة لاتربطها بها صلة قرابة، الا اذا لم يتمكن منهم أحد بالقيام بالمرافقَة. لا أحد منهم يجيد اللغة الانكليزية. جلبنا لهم رسائل بذاك الخصوص.
بعد أنْ أصدروا جواز سفري، سألتهم: "أليس ممنوعاً على النساء السفر وقت الحرب؟" فوضّحوا: "مسموح لهن حين تبعثهن الحكومة."

في الطائرة، أبدت غادة رغبتها بزيارة نصب الحرية أولاً. قلتُ لها بأننا في الطريق الى سان فرانسيسكو وليس الى نيويورك. في اليوم التالي، كنا نتمشى عند جسر الغولدن غيت نلتقط صوراً مع حمامات على الأرض. لم أكن قد رأيت قبل ذلك حمامات هكذا على الأرض مع الناس دون ذعر أو رصاص. أرادت غادة أن تشاهد فيلماً في التلفزيون، الا أنني بقيتُ أقلبُ القنوات حتى أعرف عددها. أخبرتْني غادة بأنها فقدتْ حاسة السمع عندما كانتْ في الرابعة عشر من عمرها اذ أُصيبت بالتيفوئيد والحمّى. "الاستماع الى أم كلثوم هو أكثر شيء أفتقدهُ"، كتبتْ في الدفتر.
المستشفى الذي راجعناه لعلاج غادة كان نظيفاً للغاية وخاليا من الصراصير. رأى الطبيب بأن غادة تحتاج الى عملية جراحية لزرع سماعة في أذنها. قالت ستفكر بذلك فيما بعد. لم ترجع الى المستشفى بعد ذلك اذ أبدتْ تخوفها من العملية.
في ديزني لاند، سألتْني فيما اذا كنتُ سأعود الى العراق أو أبقى في أميركا. فهمتُ بأنها كانت قلقة من امكانية تعرّضها لاستجواب أمني فيما اذا عادتْ بدوني. لكني أردت أن أعود لأني اشتقتُ الى غرفتي و عائلتي و أصدقائي ونظرة مازن التي تستقبلني حين أدخل الى أمسية الأربعاء في اتحاد الأدباء.

. . .

بعد أن تخرجتُ من الجامعة، أُدخل أبي الى المستشفى للمرة الأولى في حياته. بعد تشخيص عجز في الكلى، نصحنا الأطباء بنقله الى مستشفى ابن البيطار اذ تتوفر هناك الأجهزة الطبية لمرضه. ولكن لابد من ورقة موافقة من وزارة الصحة لتحويله الى ذاك المستشفى.

من دائرة الى أخرى

ومن قسم الى آخر

ومن وزارة الى أخرى

ومن واسطة الى أخرى

حتى وافقوا على نقلِه.

لم يكن أبي بعثياً ولم تكن له مرتبة عسكرية ولكن له "واسطة" عبر "أبو فيصل" الذي كان شريكه في الفندق والذي قطع اجازته ليساعد في موضوع الموافقة.

"تعالي غدا" هكذا يقولون لك كلما احتجتَ الى ورقة من دائرة حكومية.

"حالة والدي خطرة. هل يمكن أن تعطيني الورقة اليوم رجاءً؟" قلت.

"ذلك مستحيل..."

"الأوراق غير موقّعة بعد..."

"سأفعل مابوسعي حالما تصلني..."

كان أبي مستلقياً في الفراش بأسى. لم ينم ليلة البارحة لأن الفتاة الصغيرة بجانب سريره كانت تصرخ "ماما، ماما" ولم يأتِها أحد. غفى لوهلة في الصباح وحينما استيقظ لم يجدها في سريرها ولم يعرف فيما اذا نقلوها الى غرفة أخرى أم انها ماتت. حاولَ ألّا يبكي. لم أرَ أبي يبكي يوماً. حتى عندما ماتت أمه، خرج وأشعلَ سيجارة فحسب. لم أجد سيجارة في فمه قبل تلك المرة، ولم يدخن أبداً بعد تلك المرة. كان يحتفظ بالسجائر للضيوف فقط.

نسيتْ جدتي كل شيء قبل أن تموت ماعدا بيت طفولتها. كوّمتْ ملابسها بداخل قطعة قماش كبيرة، ربطتْها وذهبتْ تفتح الباب في منتصف الليل لأنها تريد الذهاب الى "بيت أبيها"، كما تسميه. نسيتْ جدتي أسماء الناس وعلاقتهم بها. نسيتْ بأن أخاها مات بعد دقائق من تقديم التعازي لها. وأمي صارتْ تخشى أن تقع جدتي من فوق سطح الدار اذ كانت تسير في نومها.

فوق ذلك السطح نفسه، كنا ننام في ليالي الصيف حيث اعتادتْ جدتي، قبل سنوات، أن تحكي لي قصصاً قبل النوم. عرفتُ لاحقاً بأن تلك حكايات شعبية عالمية. وأنا، الطفلة المتشوقة لسماع تلك الحكايات مرات ومرات، سألتُها فيما اذا كانت متوفرة في كتاب. كنتُ أحلم بقراءة تلك القصص بنفسي لأعيد التفاصيل وأرى الرسومات كما أشاء. وكانت تعيدُ الجواب: "أتمنى لو كانت في كتاب لأعطيك أياه. أنا سمعتُها من جدتي وهكذا ستفعلين أنت أيضاً مع أحفادك."

كلنا توقعنا موتها عندما ماتت. قبل دقيقة من موتها، أشارتْ الى السقف حيث رأتْ طيرين.

تساءلتْ أمي فيما اذا كانا طيرين أم ملاكين أتيا ليأخذاها الى الجنة.

كان أبي يحب أن يحكي لي قصصاً في أثناء قيلولة النهار. قصته المفضلة كانت عن أخوين، عجيب وغريب، تفرّقا وذهب كل منهما في طريق. تجمعهما المصادفات أحياناً ولكن لايعرف أحدهما الآخر. كان يحكي لي كل يوم جزءاً من القصة، ثم يستسلم للنوم ويشخر بعد كل التشويق الذي يثيره، ولاتفلح محاولتي في ايقاظه. أفتح عينيه بأصابعي لكنهما تنسدلان مرة أخرى.

خرجتُ من غرفته في المستشفى لأعثر على ممرضة وهرعتُ الى ثلاثة أشخاص بصدريات بيض. طبيب و طالبان جاءا ليتعلّما من حالة أبي. قال لي الطبيب، "لابد أن أخبركِ بأن حالته خطيرة."

مازلنا لانملك ورقة الموافقة لتحويله الى ابن البيطار.
غداً، غداً...

"الأمر بيد الله"، قالوا لي في الوزارة، "افرحي لأنك ستحصلين عليها في كل الأحوال. بعض الناس لا تتوفر لديهم مثل هذه الفرصة."

عدتُ الى المستشفى ولكن وقت الزيارة انتهى. ركضتُ الى المصعد. ركض موظف الاستعلامات ورائي وركض أخي خلفه. ضغطتُ زر الاغلاق بوجه الموظف.
هناك في الطابق العلوي، كان الطبيب يضغط على قلب أبي بقوة. ضربتُ بيدي على طرف السرير لأخيف صرصاراً أحمر وأبعده عن جسد أبي. نظر اليّ الطبيب تلك النظرة المشفقة.
في موقع الاستعلامات، لمحتُ أخي الأصغر الذي كان في الصف الأول الأبتدائي بعيداً عن باقي أفراد العائلة، ينظر عبر النافذة. نظرتُ الى أمي دونما كلام. أدركتْ فوراً ما حدث فبدأتْ تنتحب باللهجة الآرامية: "زال أبوكم، زال، زال."

دفعوا بأبي وهو على السرير ذي العجلات الى خارج الغرفة. سألتهُم "الى أين؟" قالوا أنهم يضعون الموتى في المجمدة الى حين الدفن.
في موقف السيارات، جلسنا على احدى العتبات لنبكي مانشاء.

النسوة بملابسهن السود ملأن منزلنا. يصغين الى تلك المرأة التي كلّفتها عمتي بأن ترتّل وتغني للميت. تتلو شعراً، حزيناً ولكن ضعيفاً. رتّلتْ كلاماً عن أمي كأرملة.

لثلاثة أيام، ظل الرجال يدخّنون في بيتنا والنساء يبكين ويولولن، يلطمن على صدورهن ويرددن أسماء شهدائهن.

في اليوم الرابع، أراد أخي الصغير أن يشاهد أفلام الكرتون ولكن عمتي اعترضتْ وقالت ان ذلك عيب. لم يكن لأمي كلمة غالباً في أي شأن. كان الأقرباء يتدخلون في حياتنا قائلين بأن موت أبينا قد كسر ظهرنا. كنتُ شعرتُ فعلاً بانكسار شيء هائل، انما تضايقتُ من عطبنا المنكشف أمام الآخرين.

عاد اليّ أبي في أحلامي. مرة يعطيني شيئاً بعد أن يكون خبأه وراء ظهره مثلما كان يفعل وأنا صغيرة، ومرة يخبرني بأنه لم يكن ميتاً عندما وضعوهُ في المجمدة. ولكنه يلتزم الصمت في معظم الأحلام.

بعد موت أبي بقليل، توقفت الحرب العراقية الأيرانية. اطلاقات نارية عشوائية في السماء، غير موجهة للقتل هذه المرة. كان ذلك في ٨– ٨– ٨٨ وقد دامت الحرب ٨ سنوات. رقم ٨ لابد انه رقم الحظ اذن. ناس مبتهجون في الشوارع وفوق سيارات تصدر منها موسيقى صاخبة. قاعات فنادق تغص بأعراس جماعية. لافتات سوداء بأسماء الشهداء، على أية حال، مازالت هناك تغطي جدران المدينة.

شعرتُ بغصة لأن أبي لم يشهد لحظة السلام تلك. مات وهو قلق على أخواني. كان يخشى أن يتخرّج أحدهم من الجامعة قبل نهاية الحرب فيُساق الى الخدمة العسكرية الألزامية. كنت أريد له أن يرى بأنهم على مايُرام.

أمي، التي تترك أمورها عادةً بيد الله، بدتْ قلقة أكثر من أي وقت مضى، حتى أكثر من اليوم الذي وقع فيه صاروخ على "سايلو" قرب كلّيتي. هي وأبي انتظراني عند باب الدار وكم تأثّرا عندما أخبرتهما بأني لم أصب بشيء. "مثلما قلتُ لك، مريم العذراء دائماً تحمي أطفالنا" قالتْ أمي لأبي "كلما فعلتم حسنات للآخرين، يحميكم الله من الخطر وأنتم حتى لاتعرفون."

بعد موت أبي، صارتْ أمي تنتظرنا عند الباب. لم أسمعها قبل ذلك تتحدث عن مخاطر العالم ماعدا تلك التي يزيلها الله مقابل حسناتنا. الآن صارتْ توصينا واحداً واحداً أن ننتبه وألا نتدخل في السياسة وألا ننتقد الحكومة، وتتحدث عن شباب وشابات يختفون عن

أعين أهلهم اذ يأخذونهم ولا يرجعون أبداً. بدأتْ أمي تقفل الباب. هي لم تفعل ذلك أبداً
من قبل عندما كان أبي على قيد الحياة، حتى انها يوماً وبخَتْني لأني قفلتُ الباب وصرختْ
بي "يا للعيب! تريدين لضيوفنا أن يطرقوا على الباب؟"
كان الضيوف يأتون الى منزلنا مراراً، وحتى بعد موت أبي، كان "قوري" الشاي برائحة
الهيل ساخناً دائماً، فلا يترك موقعه على المدفأة النفطية الا ليعود اليها كل مرة وغطاؤه
يهتز بصخب كأنه يشترك في تلك الأحاديث.

. . .

في أحد الأيام، تقدمتْ مني احدى طالبات الصف وقالت "أليس عيباً ألا تكوني واحدة منا
في حزب البعث؟ انسانة جيدة مثلك لابد أن تنتمي." اضطررتُ أن أقول لها بأنه من
الصعب حضور اجتماعات الحزب وبأنني سأفكر بالأمر عندما تتحسن ظروفي.

قبل حرب الخليج، كانت أمي تصب الشاي في أكواب الضيوف للمرة الثانية عندما قالت
احداهن "صدام أصلاً أخذ الأوكي من أمريكا بضم الكويت." وقال آخرون لن تكون هناك
حرب، لأنه سيسحب القوات في اللحظة الأخيرة فلا يعطي عذراً لأمريكا لتهجم. آخرون
توقعوا الحرب فأسعار المعلّبات ارتفعتْ تواً وكأن التجار ترقبوا وتمنوا تلك الأسعار.
وهكذا استمر كلام الحرب.

كنتُ أكره أن أستيقظ مبكرة في الصباح، ولكن في يوم ١٧ كانون الثاني، ١٩٩١، أيقظتني
أمي في الساعة الثانية صباحاً، فالحرب جاءتْ مرة أخرى. وكم تمنيتُ لو انها تمهلتْ قليلاً
حتى ننتهي من نومنا أولاً هذه المرة.

صرختْ بي أمي لأنضم اليها والى اخواني الأربعة في الغرفة الخاصة التي هيأتْها للحرب.
غطتْ النوافذ بشريط لاصق وسدّتْ به كذلك ثقب مفتاح الباب حتى لاتتسرب الى الغرفة
غازات كيمياوية. ماكان يمكننا الذهاب الى الحمام قبل انتهاء صافرة الانذار اذ قالت بأنه
يتحتم علينا أن نعيش أو نموت معاً في تلك البقعة. كانت أصوات الانفجارات ترتفع أكثر
وأكثر وكأنها تأتي أقرب وأقرب.

أخذتْ أمي تصلّي بأن "الله الممتلئ رحمة سيخلصنا." فتذكرتُ الشاعر يهودا اميخاي
الذي يقول في أحدى قصائده بأنه لو لم يكن الله ممتلئاً بالرحمة لتوفرتْ رحمةٌ في
العالم وليس لديه فقط.

حاولَ كل منا أن يشعل شمعة ولم ينجح أحد. ظلّت الشمعة تنطفيء وبدأنا نشعر باختناق في تلك الغرفة الموصدة الخالية من الاوكسجين. رنَ الهاتف من بعيد. استغربنا بأن الكهرباء لم تنقطع بعد وأن الهاتف كان مايزال يشتغل. الضوء انطفأ أولاً في الحرب السابقة وبعد ذلك كان ينطفيء في بداية كل صافرة انذار. عبر الهاتف، قال لنا الأقاربُ بأننا، اذا توفر لنا بنزين، ينبغي أن نهرب كلنا الى تلكيف اذ سمعوا بأن الأمريكان لن يقصفوا هناك. ظلتْ أمي تتحدث معهم حتى مات الهاتف أخيراً بيدها.

امتلأ بيت خالتي درّة في قرية أجدادنا بالناس والحيوانات. أبقار ودجاج وحمير تسرح وتمرح في المكان تاركة أيانا جميعاً في غرفة واحدة. يالها من محظوظة تلك الحيوانات فليس عليها أن تبالي بالحرب! ولكن مَن يدري؟ ربما أصوات الانفجارات البعيدة والطائرات المقتربة ليلاً أرعبتها، هي أيضاً.

كنا نجلس على شكل دائرة حول المذياع نستمع الى الأخبار. نغلق المذياع في بداية كل اعلان تجاري بين الأخبار وذلك لحفظ البطارية. "سننقطع عن العالم تماماً اذا ماتت هذه البطاريات، فلا يمكن العثور عليها في أي مكان اللهم بمبلغ يمكن للمرء أن يتزوج به"، قال ابن خالتي وهو يحمل كيساً هائلاً من الطحين. نفد بعد اسبوع واحد لأن خالتي استخدمتهُ لاطعامنا جميعاً. كان وجهها أحمر طوال الوقت الذي مكثتْ قربه اذ ظلتْ تخبز و تخبز و تخبز. المرة الوحيدة التي حاولتْ فيها أن تشارك في أحاديث السياسة، قالتْ "أعتقد أن بوش لن يقصف تلكيف فالكثير من الكلدان هنا لديهم أقارب في أميركا."

في الليل، كنا نشعر ببرد شديد فلايمكن اشعال مدفأة لأن الغاز غير متوفر. ولكن البرد كان سيشتد أكثر لولا كل تلك الأجساد المحيطة بك. لم يجرؤ أحد أن يتذكر الاستحمام فلم يكن ذلك لائقاً مع شحة الماء. وضعتْ خالتي سطلاً تحت المطر، ولكنها لم تتمكّن من استخدامه اذ كان اسود، مطراً أسود.

المذياع بثّ خبراً عن قصف محطات الكهرباء في بغداد. تذكرتْ أمي بأنها كانت قد ملأتْ المجمدة بالطعام تحضيراً لوقت الحرب. تضايقتْ كثيراً من التفكير بالطعام وهو يتعفّن. "كيف نسينا أن نجلب الطعام؟ كيف غادرنا هكذا دون أن نجلب شيئاً؟" تساءلتْ عشر مرات.

بعد عشرة أيام، قررنا العودة الى بغداد بالرغم من أخبار القصف الشديد على العاصمة.

84

حذَّرَنا ابن خالتي قائلاً: "هل أنتم مجانين؟ قد لا تجدون بيتكم في محلّه اذا وصلتم. هنا تسمعون أصوات الطائرات فقط. هناك ستسمعون أصوات الغارات والقصف ليل نهار."

صدع كبير على الجدار الذي يفصل بيننا والجيران هو أول شيء لاحظناه. الجدار الذي لم نبالِ باصلاحه حتى عندما سقط فجأة بعد الحرب.

في البيت، شعرتُ بترف شم زهور الرازقي كلما مررت من عند الحديقة بالرغم من الشظايا المبعثرة على الحشيش. استمتعتُ بالاستحمام بالرغم من اضطراري الى عد قطرات الماء الشحيحة. وشعرتُ بسعادة أن أكون في سريري برفقة كتاب ولو اهتزت الأرض تحت السرير من القصف وقراءتي قاطعتْها صافرات الانذار، ولكن سمحتْ لنا أمي بالنوم في أسرّتنا. شعرنا بأننا في البيت، بيتنا بامتياز.

ونحن نحتسي الشاي، عبّرتْ أمي عن دهشتها كيف جعلَها الأمريكيون (بوصفهم بالنسبة لها مسيحيون أتقياء) ترمي طعامها المجمّد في كيس الزبالة بعد أن أمضت كل ذلك الوقت في صنعه. لم تدخل المعلبات بيتنا قبل ذلك اذ كانت أمي تفخر وتستمتع دائماً بعمل وجباتها المعقدة. تنهض في الصباح الباكر لتحضير لوازم تلك الوجبات. تبدو بمنتهى الجدية وهي تمزج التوابل والأطعمة. كميات هائلة من الطعام تشعرك بوجود حملة في المطبخ. في المساءات، كل الجيران بالاضافة الى الأصدقاء والأقارب سيتذوقون الطعام الذي هي معروفة به. ولكن "أم المعارك" عرّفتنا الى المعلبات. وجدناها لذيذة برغم التعليب وبرغم أو بسبب كميتها القليلة. لم نكن نريدها أن تنفذ قبل انتهاء الحرب لأن سيارتنا باتت بلا بنزين والدكان الوحيد القريب من منزلنا كان مغلقاً. استخدم "عمّو" كل معلبات الدكان لاطعام عائلته الكبيرة. زوجته وأبناؤه الثلاثة وزوجاتهم وأطفالهم بالاضافة الى أبويه يعيشون معه.

بعد أربعين يوماً، أُعلن وقف اطلاق النار. دُعي الجنود العراقيون الى الانسحاب من الكويت. عاد بعضهم مشياً على الأقدام، بعضهم حفاة، وبعضهم قُتل في الطريق من قبل قوات الحلفاء. دُعي الموظفون الى العودة لوظائفهم وأُعلنتْ حملة لأعادة الاعمار.

تجنّبْنا المرور بالجسور في طريقنا الى العمل لأنها كانت مهدّمة. لم نستخدم الهاتف فدوائر الاتصالات تمّ قصفها. توفرت لنا كهرباء لبضع ساعات في اليوم، والطيور لم تعد تعثّر على أسلاك تقف عليها. كانت العقوبات الاقتصادية ماتزال مفروضة على العراق مختزلة كل شيء الى حجم أصغر وأصغر، خبزاً أم كتاباً. شحة الورق أدّت بابن خالتي الى أن يمزق كتبي (الكتب التي كنتُ تركتها لديه) ليف بأوراقها حبات الفلافل التي كان

يبيعها في محلّهِ.

عبد الأمير جرص بعثَ لي كتابه الشعري الذي كان بحجم علبة ثقاب. كتبتُ قصائد حرب جديدة، هذه المرة على كلتا صفحتي الورقة. كانت أمي جالسة على الأرض حافية القدمين، تقرأ قصيدتي (ضمائر منفصلة) التي كانت منشورة ذلك اليوم في الجريدة. تلك كانت المرة الأولى التي أراها تقرأ لي فشعرتُ باضطراب شديد. "هو يلعب قطاراً، هي تلعب صفارة، هم يرحلون"، أخذتْ تقرأ. ثم قالت "أعتقد ان الأطفال سيعجبهم هذا الشعر."

- "لماذا الأطفال؟"

- "أ ليس هذا للأطفال؟"

- "لستُ متأكدة"

أخبرتْني كم هي فخور بي وكيف انني حين ولدتُ بكتْ عمّاتي لأنني بنت وأنهن شعرنَ بالأسف لأبي لأنه طيب و يستحقُ ولداً وليس بنتاً. ولكن لم يدم حزنهن أكثر من سنتين حيث وُلد أخي الكبير فاستقبلنهُ بالتهاني والزغاريد. ولكن لم يخبروهن في المستشفى أي شيءٍ عن تخلفه العقلي.

تركتُ أمي وصعدتُ الى غرفتي. كتبتُ:

أمي تنجب بنتاً
بينما الجميع ينتظر ولداً
فيقابلونها بتجهم وفتور
والبنت ليس بمقدورها العودة
من حيث أتتْ
فتنحني مثل قوس
وتبدأ بكاءها الأول.

تعطيها الأم دفتراً وقلماً
لتلهيها عن العالم
البنت ترسم نفسها وردةً
يمر بها عاشقٌ
ويقطفها لحبيبته
يتحدثان عن تجفيفها في كتاب
وهما يسيران جنباً الى جنب

والوردة تفكر:
كيف سأتحمل ذاك الجفاف المؤبد
بين ورقتي الكتاب؟

تقلب صفحة الدفتر
وترسم نفسها ساعة
تدق للآخرين
وترتعش في مواعيد محددة
أحدهم يريدها أن توقظه في الصباح الباكر جداً
آخر يهدد بالتخلص منها
اذا لم تكن مضبوطة تماماً.
في منتصف الليل
يتعانق عقرباها وينسيان العالم.

تقلب الصفحة ثانيةً
وترسم نفسها كنزاً
في حلم أحدهم
ولكن تختفي حينما يستيقظ.
ترسم نفسها لطخة
و تجلس في كتاب التاريخ
الى جانب زميلاتها اللطخات
كم مرعب أن ترى تلك الفرشاة الضخمة
التي يحملها فريق عمل بكامله
لتلميع الصفحات.

ترسم نفسها شجرة
انه يدغدغها
ذلك العصفور وهو يبني عشه
على غصنها
تضحكُ فتتساقط ثمارها
يمرّ من تحت أوراقها
أشكال وألوان من البشر

منهم مَن يخرمشها
وهو يخط اسمين على جذعها
مع سهم كيوبيد
وآخر يهرع اليها بفأسهِ
ذاك القفصُ هناك
ينتمي اليها
والطير الذي بداخلهِ
يبدو أليفاً بالنسبة لها .

تقلب الصفحة
وترسم نفسها شمساً
تقسم وقتها بين الجميع بالتساوي
مشكلتها أنها تحتاج الى عطلة
ترسم نفسها ممحاة
وتمرّ على كل صفحات الدفتر
ترجعهُ لأمها
نظيفاً مثلما كان
لعلها تُرسم من جديد
ولكن جُلَّ ماتخشاه
أن تُرسم ولداً
فتذهب الى الجندية.

. . .

كنتُ كل يوم أحمدُ الله لأنه خلقني بنتاً ، فلم أُدعَ الى الخدمة العسكرية. لم أضطر الى
قتل أحد ولم يطالبني أحد بهويتي وأنا في الشارع. انما تمددتُ ببساطة في سريري وأنا
أستمع الى الموسيقى وليس الى أصوات قادة عسكريين "أشداء ولايرحمون" كما قال
مازن.

لم أستلم منه رسالة بعد. هل يدري بأني غيرتُ عنواني؟
في مكتب البريد في بغداد، قيل لي بأني لابد كنتُ مدللة لأطلب أن تُحَوّلَ الرسائل الى
عنواني الجديد. "يجب أن تخبريهم عن عنوانك الجديد بنفسك،" قال موظف البريد.

غياب مازن أقلقني، وغياب أبي أقلقَ أمي. كانت تروح وتجيء بين الباب و طاولة المطبخ أو تجلسُ وهي تحدق بي.

وفي يوم، حضرتُ اجتماعاً غريباً في مسرح ساحة الاحتفالات. كان قد جاءنا بلاغ (الى الصحفيين كافة) باجتماع اجباري مع عدي (ابن صدام). بدأ كل واحد منا يحاول تخمين السبب. "يقال بأن هناك مكرمة للصحفيين"، تناقل الخبر بيننا بسرعة مثل أي اشاعة أخرى. جلسنا هناك في انتظار الاجتماع الغامض والمفاجيء. على المنصة أمامنا جلس رجلان بصمت. أحدهما مدير تحرير جريدة الجمهورية والآخر مدير تحرير جريدة القادسية. وجلس المقعد الثالث فارغاً بانتظار عدي. بعد ساعة أو أكثر، جاء شخص عابس نحيف وجلس على الكرسي الثالث. وضع ورقة أمامه وقرأ: عدي يحييكم وينقل اليكم هذه الرسالة. ألقى الرجل علينا محاضرة اخلاقية طويلة بخصوص المواطنة والاخلاص والخيانة ختمَها بقوله انّ الرجلين على المنصة خائنان للوطن. بدأ أحد الأشخاص في مقعد أمامي يرميهما فوراً بالزبالة. بعد ذلك مباشرة، ظهر شخصان مسلحان وأخذا المديرَين تاركين المنصة الحمراء الأنيقة خاوية وهازئة من جبننا جميعاً نحن الصحفيين الذين خرجنا من القاعة دون أن ننبس بكلمة. بدأتُ بالبحث عن سيارتي اذ نسيتُ أين أوقفتُها وأنا أنظر الى الجموع المتفرقة بوجوهها المصفرّة وقرونها (قرون الخراف) التي نبتت لنا على حين غرة. تمشيتُ وحدي في مظاهرة صامتة وأنا أفكر مَن ياترى جلب زبالة الى القاعة المخصصة للاحتفالات أو للمسرحيات التي لاتشبه مسرحية اليوم؟ فحتى مسرحيات شكسبير المليئة بالقتل تنتهي، بعد أن يسدل الستار، بالشخوص كلهم ممسكين أيدي بعضهم البعض، القاتل والقتيل معاً يحنيان رأسيهما لتحيتنا. ذكّرَني الحدث بحكاية شعبية بغيضة عن عريس يقتل قطة أمام العروس في يوم العرس حتى يجعلها تخافه مدى الحياة.

عدتُ الى البيت لأضطجع فوراً في الفراش حتى الصباح. لم أذهب الى الجريدة في اليوم التالي. سألتني أمي فيما اذا كنتُ مريضة فقلت لها اني لا أنوي الذهاب الى الجريدة بعد ذلك. رويتُ لها ماحدث بعد أن أصرّت أن تعرف السبب. ذكّرتني بأنهُ لم يكن مسموحاً للموظفين بترك العمل من دون "معاملة" ودفع نفقات الدراسة. بعد اسبوع، اتصلتْ بي هدى وأخبرتني بانها قدّمتْ لي اجازة مرضية وان الاجازة على وشك أن تنتهي. رجعتُ الى العمل متنازلة عن احتجاجي مثلما سأتنازل بعد ذلك عن وطني كله. شعرتُ بأني في منفى مزيّف، أتوق لمنفى حقيقي.

تصورتُ، لحظة الرحيل، بأني أملك وقتاً لتوديع أصدقائي أو لحضور حفلة زفاف أخي في

الأسبوعين القادمين. "لا. لابد أن ترحلي فوراً. حياتك أهم من حضور حفلتي. سنبعث لكِ الفيديو لاحقاً." قال لي.

لطفية قالت، "لقد أخبرتك، ذلك النص الذي نشرتهِ عن زيوس كان خطيراً. كنتِ تعرفين ذلك ولكن تتجاهلين. هل تظنين لهم قلوباً؟ لا. هم يؤذون من شاءوا دون أن يفكروا بذلك مرتين."

. . .

في الخارج، صرتُ أرى نفسي في الحلم عائدة الى وطني، أراني نادمة مضطربة وغير واثقة من امكانية خروجي بأمان مرة أخرى. في أحلام أخرى، أشعر بالنشوة اذ أفاجىء أصدقائي بعودتي. أحياناً لا أتذكّر أحلامي.

يوقظني المنبه للعمل باكراً. تتكدس أوراق الخريف الصفراء والحمراء والبنية في مشيفان تحت أقدام الأطفال الذاهبين الى المدرسة. عليّ أن أصل قبلهم حتى أتهيأ لهم، أرتّب غرفة الصف، وأستقبلهم عند الباب. طلابي أكثرهم من أصول عربية. يعرفون التحدث بالعربية ولكنهم لايعرفون القراءة والكتابة بها. نفتح الكتاب من اليمين الى اليسار، فيعلّقُ بعض الطلاب بأن "هذه لغة بالمقلوب."

الصف تعمّهُ فوضى وأصوات عالية وقوانين منتهَكة وممحاة تتركُ آثاراً على الورقة. لا أعرف كيف أتشدّد مع المراهقين. صفي يشبه بلداً محتلاً.

كنتُ أعمل في مكتبة "بوردرز" عندما أرادتني لويس أن أشتغل مساعدة في برنامج مدرسي ثنائي اللغة، كانتْ مشرفة عليه. لم أتردد بترك عملي، ولكنني حين باشرتُ العمل في الصف، شعرتُ بأني كنتُ أقاطع المدرّسين مراراً وأنا أترجم للطلاب القادمين الجدد. فضّلتُ أن أملك صفي الخاص. بعدئذ، عندما مُنحتُ صفاً، صرتُ أتحدث وطلابي يقاطعونني.

كانت لويس تربّي في بيتها ست قطط. عرّفتني الى خمس منهم فالسادسة خجولة جداً، ولن تظهر أمام الغرباء. في كيس الصور، لويس تلتقط التوت من شجيرة في حديقتها.

انتهى مفعول ورقة القبول الصفراء من جامعة "وين ستيت" اذ تأخّرتُ خمس عشرة سنة.

أعطوني استمارة جديدة. باشرتُ الدراسة في الجامعة وقد وجدتُها مختلفة تماماً عن جامعة بغداد. فالآن أحضر الدروس دون أن أعرف أسماء الطلاب الذين معي في الصف. لا نتجمّع لنتحدث بعد الدرس. لانأكل "اللبلبي" من عربة بائع متجول في الباحة. لانذهب في نزهة طلابية الى مدينة الألعاب. لانرتدي الزي الموحد الأبيض والرمادي والأزرق. لانُأخذُ الى المظاهرات. نوافذ الصف لا تهتز من صواريخ سقطتْ في مكان ما، مثلما سقطت كل مرة في بغداد. ومازن لم يكن هناك.

ولكن عملية التخاطر بيننا نجحتْ هذه المرة فقد عثرتْ عليّ رسالتُه، ولو تجولتْ حول العالم عشر سنوات قبل أن تصلني. ولكنها وصلتْني ولم ينتهِ مفعولها. فتحتُها كمن يفتح أحشاء سمكة يعرف أن خاتمه في أحشائها.

كان يبعث الرسائل الى عنواني القديم في العراق. ولكن عندما رأى يوماً قصيدتي "خروج الأصدقاء" منشورة في جريدة عربية في لندن، اتصل بهم يسأل عن عنواني. مثل رسالة في انبوبة رُميتْ في البحر، رسالته تجولتْ من قارة الى أخرى، من شخص الى آخر، حتى وصلتْ الى هدى في العراق فبعثتْها الى مشيغان. كانت قادمة في الأصل من أستراليا مع طابع عليه صورة كنغر.

جاء مازن الى ديترويت. عانقني في المطار وقد كبرَ كثيراً وشعرهُ تغيرَ الى اللون الرمادي وقد تساقط نصفه. شعري لم يتغير فقد صبغتهُ. قال، "لم أصدق عيني عندما جاءني منك جواب أخيراً" وأضاف، "لم أصدّق انك لم تتزوجي بعد فقد كبرتِ."
"وأنتَ كذلك"، أجبتُ.
"قرأتُ رسالتك عشر مرات"، قال.
"و أنا كذلك!"، أجبت.

لقاؤنا صادف في يوم كذبة نيسان. كان ينبغي أن يغادر خلال ثلاثة أشهر حسب تأشيرة الزيارة الممنوحة له، فلم يُرتكب أي خطأ في جواز سفره. ولأننا لم نتزوج قبل منحي اللجوء، لم يستطع أن يقيم رسمياً في الولايات المتحدة الا بعد حصولي على الجنسية الأمريكية وعندذاك نتزوج.

ماكنتُ سأصبح مواطنة قبل عشر سنوات أخرى! كانوا يريدوننا أن ننتظرعشر سنوات فهم لايالون بالسنوات العشر الضائعة التي سبقتها.

ذكرتْ لي لوري بأن ثمة اقامة استثنائية تُمنح للأدباء "الموهوبين" وعوائلهم. قالتْ، "جرّبي فأنتِ شاعرة متميزة ومن المؤمل أن يعرفوا ذلك."
جرّبتُ فعلاً وبعثتُ استمارة التقديم مع ملحق سميك يضم أرشيفي الأدبي. كان مبعثراً

دائماً لكني قمتُ بترتيبه لذلك الغرض. وصلني الجواب بالرفض مع توضيح للسبب بأنني لم أحصل على جائزة نوبل أو مايوازيها من جوائز. ضحكنا. "جائزة نوبل لاتأتي عادةً الا بعد فوات الأوان," قلتُ.

كان وصولي الى أميركا قد تأجل ١٢ سنة. دراستي في جامعة "وين ستيت" تأجلتْ ١٥ سنة. زواجي تأجل ١٠ سنوات. لم أستطع تكلّف المزيد من التأجيلات. تمنيتُ للحظة أن أترك بلد القوانين وأعود الى بلد اللا قوانين. كم كان سيساعدني أصدقائي ويعملون لي "واسطة." كم رأيتهم يغامرون بما تبقّى من النار في أرواحهم لاشعال آخر عود ثقاب في هذه العلبة الفارغة فراغ قبر أنكر النازلون اليه موتّهم في اللحظة الأخيرة، ولكن الوهج مازال هناك يدلّ.

. . .

واصلْنا غيابنا، بمختلف الألوان والصور، ونحن ندحرج أغنيتنا مثل عجلة مسرعة بلا عينين، تجرّنا وراءها أينما تشاء. كنا ندري أن مصباح علاء الدين انطفأ في ايدينا ونحن نهرع لتفحّص ظلماتنا المتوهجة هناك، في ماوراء الأشياء، في أكثرها فاعلية وحلماً وطفولة. نواصل، نواصل مسعانا، لانقاذ احدنا الآخر فما عادت لنا طاقة لأنقاذ العالم وقد كبرنا، كبرنا حد اننا لا نريد سوى أن يتركنا العالم وشأننا.

انها منعشة هذه الصابونة الجديدة التي عثرتُ عليها ولكنها لاتغسل مافات ولاتزيل عنا رائحة البارود.

أعتذرُ لأني تركتكم بين الأنقاض.
أعتذرُ لأني تركتكم دونما وداع.
أعتذرُ للمكان الجديد لأني حملتُ أنقاضي معي.
أعتذرُ لأني لم أستطع أن أكون في مكان وفي مكان آخر في الوقت نفسه.
أعتذرُ من الحرب لأني تجاهلتُ كوابيسها بأن أدرتُ وجهي الى الجهة الأخرى.
أعتذرُ من صفارات الانذار لأني فضّلتُ عليها صوت الموسيقى وايقاع النافورات.
أعتذرُ لأني أركض لتخفيف الوزن بدلاً من تلك الاندفاعات العشوائية لدى سماع أصوات الانفجارات.
أعتذرُ، أعتذرُ منكم ياأصدقائي لأني تركتكم وانشغلتُ عن آلامكم. الحياة تستمر من وراء ظهوركم. أعتذر.

بعيدا عنكم، أركّز نظري على البقع السماوية القليلة المتناثرة بين قمم ناطحات السحاب في أميركا ذات بطاقات الائتمان واليانصيب والوجبات السريعة.

أرحل عنكم وأنا أحبكم.

نندهش اذ يضيء العالم لنا وينطفيء، يربطنا به ويفصلنا عنه على نحوٍ ما، مثل أضواء شجرة الميلاد. وأحلامنا تُقلب طوال الوقت مثل أوراق التقاويم التي تتوالى ابتساماتٍ أليفة. نكبرُ ولا يكبر موتانا ولا الذكريات. يمسّنا الشعرُ فنتوهج للحياة، من أجلها وربما برغمها.

كنتُ سمكةً قبل أن أُسحر الى انسان. لذلك أحنّ أحياناً الى حياتي السابقة وحركتي الحرة في الماء. أختنق أحياناً على اليابسة.

أعتذر من البريد العادي لأني الآن أفضّل الأيميل. يعجبني كيف انكم على بعد نقرة ولو الأمر مختلف تماماً. يعجبني كيف استطاع فأر الكومبيوتر أن يتحكم بالعالم أخيراً. أن تغلق نافذة لايعني انك ألغيتها اذ يمكنك استدعاءها متى شئت لتتقدم نوافذك الاخرى المفتوحة أو المغلقة تواً. كل شيء، حتى العراق، موجود هناك (لايمكن الغاؤه حتى بالخطأ)، محفوظ في مكان ما بعدة نسخ مكبّراً أو مصغّراً في صور وايقونات وأفكار وأحداث وناس، صندوق بندورا غير مفتوح، بداخله أصدقائي يحملون كتباً مستعملة من شارع المتنبي، أو رائحة سمك مسكوف أو شاي بالهيل يغلي مثل تراب أليف. في ضفة أخرى، السلحفاة والأرنب تركا ساحة السباق بعد أن اكتشفا بأن ثمة أمراً أهم من ذلك.

يتحرك الفأر فتنفتح ايقونة الأرقام الشاعرة. وقع نظري عليها لدى وصولي الى أميركا. أعجبتني الشفرات الرياضية ترن أو تتذبذب برسائل رومانسية أو تجارية أو لاأدرية. ١٤٣ بمعنى "أحبك"، ١٨٧ بمعنى " أقتلك"، ١٨٧-٢-١٤٣ بمعنى "أحبك حتى الموت." الانسان تظل به حاجة الى العاطفة حتى في أحشاء التكنلوجيا.

للكلمات حيوات سرية، حيوية وزئبقية، خارج أوراقنا. ولها ميتات متعاقبة ونسيانات فادحة وقبائل لاتدري لماذا تهاجر ولماذا لاتهاجر. مرنةٌ هي ومستعدة للتخلي عن اسمها أو فعلها الأصلي من أجل ارضائنا. بل انها تنهض من جديد بمجرد اشارة تومض في أذهاننا. "المنفى" مثلاً كلمة مختلفة الألوان والتداعيات، وفاعلها كائن يحس بشوق ما مع كل حركة.

يتحرك الفأر فتنفتح أيقونة الرقص:

الايقاع يحرّرنا من كل رقابة. يبعث الرقصُ، من خلال النشوة، نبضاتٍ متموجةً فيستيقظ الكون. الحركة المنسابة للكون تنجز الظاهرة المتنوعة الأبعاد. هكذا نرقص تلك الرقصة الكونية في الفراغ ونحن نكتب. اذا راقبنا حركاتنا، نتعثر فتخرب الرقصة. حينما نذهب للنوم، ربما تصحو الأشباح وتقيم رقصاتها. ربما تتشاجر أو تسكر أو تتبادل الشتائم. ربما تكافح من أجل اثبات وجودها. ولكننا لا ندري. فنحن، كأي آلهة مشغولين، نشاهد التلفزيون ونقرأ الجرائد ونمتنُ لأن ماحدث لم يحدث لنا.

تنط هذه الحكايات عندما يتحرك الفأر:

الضفدعة و الملك
كانت هناك ضفدعة كلما قفزتْ في ذهن الملك ، تقوم الحرب. وقد احتار الشعبُ بأمر هذه الضفدعة العجيبة التي لايمكن القضاء عليها ولا الحد من قفزاتها المتعاقبة. ولما تنامى عدد اليتامى والأرامل، عُقدتْ اجتماعات لاقناع الضفدعة بالعدول عن القفز أو على الأقل لتقفز في مكان آخر، خارج ذهن الملك. "يا لهُ من ملك مسكين" قالوا "ليس الأمر بيده..."

كلام القمر
كان القمر في السماء يحاور القمر الذي في النهر. الأول كان وحيداً وطلب من الثاني أن يصعد اليه من أجل السمر. قال، "ليس عندي مَن أبوح له بأسراري. كل ذرة في الكون مشغولة بمحيطها وأنا أطل على الأشياء ولا أندمج فيها. بي حاجة الى صديق." ولكن القمر الذي في النهر اكتفى بالتموّج والتمايل. قال القمر العالي أخيراً "حسناً، سأنزل أليك أنا اذن مادمتَ لاتستطيع الصعود. النزول دائماً أسهل من الصعود على أية حال." وهكذا قفز القمر الى النهر تلك القفزة التي سلّمتهُ لمختلف التيارات المتدافعة. لم يعرف الحقيقة الّا في الظلمة.

الكرة الطائرةُ
كانت الكرة تتقافز بين أيدي اللاعبين. يرمي بها أحدهم الى الآخر ويحاول كم منهم الامساك بها وضربها. وهي، الكرة الطائرة، فزعة من هذا الحشد من الأيدي والأقدام التي تلاحقها، ليس لها الا أن تروح وتجيء وفق حركاتهم، في انتظار أن تنط بعيداً الى الطرقات الواسعة الطليقة لتلامس الأرضَ بخفة وهدوء وكأنها في حضن حبيب. ركضَ اليها، من الجانب الآخر، صبي صغير فأخذها الى مكان محدّد بجدران أربعة. لم تتذمر الكرةَ من وضعها الجديد غير انها تتخيّل عالماً خارج الجدران فحسب.

المرآة

كل الصور التي عشناها تظهر خلفنا في المرآة، في الاتجاه الزجاجي المعاكس. أعراس، حروب، جنس، جرائم، قهقهات، تضغنات. المرآة تتلقى كل مايقفز اليها من مشاهد وهي ماكثة هناك، لاتدري بأن انكساراً واحداً، مثلا، يكفي ليشظّي كل شيء.

الأرض القديمة

كان ياما كان في يوم من الأيام...

تقدمت الأرض الجديدة من الأرض القديمة وقالت، "انظري، أنا جئتُ لأخلّصكِ. بكِ حاجة الى دم جديد."

قالت الأرض القديمة، "آه، ولكني مليئة بالدم توأً. مثلما ترين، الدم هنا في كل مكان:

في الأنهار

على التراب

تحت البنايات

في البيوت

في المستشفيات."

قالت الأرض الجديدة، "أقصد تحتاجين الى تجديد. لذلك أبعثُ اليكِ أبنائي وبناتي. سيعبرون البحار و الصحارى ليصلوا اليك. سنصحّيكِ من النوم لنمنحكِ "بريزنت"."

تساءلت الأرض القديمة، "بريزنت"؟ الحاضرُ؟ أنا أعيش في الماضي فقط."

قالت الأرض الجديدة، "بريزنت هدية. شيء يُسمى ديمقراطية."

قالت الأرض القديمة، "لحد الآن لم أجد غير الوعد بها."

قالت الأرض الجديدة، "لم تعرفي كيف تستلمينها. خرّبتها."

قالت الأرض القديمة، "أنا معتادة على الخرائب. فأنا أصنع المزيد منها كل مرّة."

. . .

قلبُ الحبيب، أينما كان، دائماً تحجبهُ عنا طبقاتُ الجلد. نحتاجُ الى عرّاف يخبرنا بأن الحرب ستنتهي والحبيب سيرجع والحزن سيزول والشمس لن تغيب أكثر وأنّ رؤساء العالم سينقلبون الى أناس طيبين حكماء يترددون قليلاً قبل أن يبدأوا الهجوم. نحتاجُ الى تعويذة تقي الأيدي الصغيرة من الأيدي الكبيرة التي تمسك السلاح.

تصورتُ أن حفلة زفافي مع مازن ستكون حدثاً ساحراً. ولكن ثوبي الأبيض كان طويلاً جداً ومقيّداً لحركتي. كانت الحفلة مملة والفرقة الموسيقية سيئة الأداء تماماً. كل شيء تم

اختيارهُ على عجل وانتقاد من الأقارب. الكل ترك الحفلة باكراً لأنه كان يوم أربعاء وليس عطلة نهاية الأسبوع. لوري جاءت من المطار مباشرة الى قاعة العرس، ولويس مع زوجها جيم جلبا يمامتين بيضاءتين أُطلقتا في القاعة ثم الى الأفق. كان جميلاً رؤية اليمامتين تطيران بعيداً، الى موطنهما الأصلي.

سبّبَ زواجنا مشاكل مع دائرة الهجرة ولكن به حظينا بابنتنا لارسا. هو اسم مدينة عراقية قديمة والاهة الشمس.

. . .

أميركا هي قارة طفلة ولا تقصد فعلاً أن تُحدث مشاكل. انما دائماً تتصور أن تبديل المشاكل أسهل من حلّها. رجل التأمين قال لي: "غسالتك عاطلة. تبديلها أسهل من تصليحها." السياسيّ قال: "بلدك مكسور. تبديلهُ أسهل من تصليحه."

أميركا تُلقي القنابل بيد وتمنحُ ملجأً باليد الأخرى.

كان يصعب على الناس في بلدي الكبير الجديد أن يعثروا على بلدي الصغير القديم في الخريطة. ولكن الحرب جعلتهُ مشهوراً وأخباره في كل مكان. صوره على أغلفة المجلات مثل نجوم هوليود. يستخدم الأمريكيون عبارات ايجابية في أسوأ الظروف فمن السهل أن تكون متفائلاً وأنت شاب.

بوش الابن تبع خطى أبيه فبدأ فترته الرئاسية بهجوم على العراق.

الأب والابن، وكلنتون هو الروح القدس فهجومهُ على العراق كان صغيراً بالمقارنة.

صدام وبوش كلاهما وعدا العراقيين بالنصر.

رُفعت العقوبات عن العراق ولكن العراقيين لايالون مادام، في الحالتين، يقفون في طوابير طويلة من أجل النفط والغاز. يذهبون الى الانتخابات و تُصبَغ أصابعهم. يقولون بأن هؤلاء المرَشَحين كلهم عملاء ولكنهم أحسن من صدام. يذهب الوزراء الجدد الى عملهم صباحاً، وبعد الظهر يخرجون في مسيرات لطم على الوجوه.

لم يعد للرقباء مكاتب انما أسلحة.

أطفال يبيعون ثلجاً على وشك أن يذوب، وكبارُ يبيعون أطفالاً.

يهرب السجناء من زنزاناتهم، البريئون منهم والمجرمون على حد سواء. يتخبطون في قمامة هائلة تملأ المدينة من الأرض الى السماء.

نهّابون يسرقون حيوانات من الحديقة. ليس بمقدور الحيوانات أن تُحدث في الشوارع ذلك الأذى الذي أحدثهُ بعض الناس.

كائنات ملثّمة تقف بسيوفها وراء رهائن مختطفة.

جنود أميركيون يتعلّمون بعض العبارات باللهجة العراقية:

أَكل

خَطَر

إرفعوا إيديكم

نزّلوا ايديكم

احجي على كيفك

لا تحجي

انبطاح

وين جرحك؟

منو المسؤول؟

أبو تحسين يضرب صورة صدام بنعاله قائلاً: "لماذا؟ لماذا فعلتَ بنا ذلك؟"
صدام يتفاوض على طريقة اعدامهِ فهو يريد أن يموت رمياً بالرصاص وليس شنقاً.

هواتف نقالة تشيع وتمررُ رسائلَ للغزل أو للتهديد أو للخطف أو للتفجير الانتحاري.

مقاهي الانترنيت تزدحم بعراقيين يبعثون "ايميلات" الى معارفهم ليساعدونهم في الخروج
من البلد. بنت الجيران القديمة تخبرني ان عصابة اختطفت زوجها وتهدد بقتله ان لم تدفع
لهم خمسين ألف دولار. ولكنها فاوضتهم وقد قبلوا بثلاثين ألف. ابنة عمتي تخبرنا انهم
حبسوا أنفسهم في البيت فلايخرجون حتى الى السوق انما هناك شخص يتسوق لبيوت
الشارع كله مقابل أجرة.

لطفية الدليمي مُنحتْ لجوءاً في فرنسا بعد تعرّضها لتهديد من قبل متديّنين متطرفيين.
تقول، "هذه ليست مدينتنا بغداد. لقد أكلها الذئب."

سهام جبار أصابتْها طلقة طائشة في الكتف. "ذلك عادي،" تقول لي عبر الهاتف.

عدنان الصائغ عاد الى البلد ليلقي شعراً في اتحاد الأدباء ولكنه غادر بعد أن تلقّى
تهديداً من أحد الواعظين.

لم تعد بغداد مقسمة الى كرخ ورصافة، وانما الى منطقة خضراء وأخرى حمراء،

ومابينهما جنود أميركيون محبطون لأن السكان لم يستقبلوهم بالزهور.

عراقيون، في كل أنحاء العالم، خرجوا الى الشوارع محتفلين ورافعين العلم لأن المنتخب العراقي لكرة القدم حاز على كأس آسيا. صرخوا بفرح في اللحظة نفسها، لحظة تسجيل الهدف، فنسوا للحظة اختلافاتهم الطائفية.

مازن يحني رأسه الى الطاولة ويبكي بكاءً مراً. ابنة أخيه اختُطفت في بغداد. عمرها عشرون سنة. حاصرها رجال ملثمون وسحبوها من يد أمها الممدودة الى سيارتهم، مثل سونامي. العراق هو سونامي ولكن بالحركة البطيئة.
أستفيق في الليل وأنا أفكّر بها: ياترى، ماذا تفعل الآن؟ أي ضيق تعيش اذا كانت تعيش؟ أن تكون في قفص تلك الأيدي الغريبة ينبغي أن يكون مجرد كابوس.

شعور هائل بالراحة ينتابني لأن بقربي ابنتي
لأنها بعيدة عن الخطر
عن غيوم مكدسة كالجثث
عن رؤوسهم الملثمة
عن الطوابير الطويلة في دائرة الجوازات
عن تلك الأصابع المبتورة في الرمل.

لارسا تبعثرُ الصور القديمة وتخلطها مع الصور الجديدة.
تخلطُ صورَ كراتِ الثلج في مشيغان مع صور مدينة مدوّرة بنهرين
ونخل
وشعر
وحروب
وألف ليلة وليلة.
بداخل تلك المدينة كان بيتنا
بداخل البيت حديقة لايفصلها جدار عن حديقة الجيران
بداخل الحديقة زهرة رازقي لن أشمّها أبداً.